CW00539426

40 Coast &
Country Walks

published by
pocket mountains ltd
The Old Church, Annanside,
Moffat DG10 9HB

ISBN: 978-1-907025-78-5

Text copyright © Paul Boobyer 2021, photography copyright © Lorna Anness

The right of Paul Boobyer to be identified as the Author of this work has been asserted by him in accordance with the Copyright, Designs and Patents Act 1988

A catalogue record for this book is available from the British Library

Contains Ordnance Survey data © Crown copyright and database 2021 supported by out of copyright mapping 1945-1961

Printed in Poland

Introduction

With a network of more than 4800km of rights of way and two national parks, Hampshire offers endless adventures for walkers. The jewel in the county's crown is the New Forest, one of Britain's most stunning national parks and a remarkable example of a medieval hunting forest. The South Downs, England's newest national park, also contains some outstanding walks in a landscape of high ecological and scenic value. With the national parks covering around 45 percent of the county, it will be no surprise that many of the walks in this volume are found within the parks, but there are less-visited gems to be explored beyond their boundaries too.

These routes are mostly easy to moderate and have been chosen to showcase Hampshire's scenic diversity, which includes forests, downlands, farmland, heaths, lakes and coast. All of the walks are on public rights of way or land with permitted access.

History

Like much of Britain, the area that was to become Hampshire was recolonised by deciduous woodland after the withdrawal of ice sheets around 10,000 years ago. As human populations grew and small settlements appeared, some forests were cleared for cultivation from at least the Bronze Age (3200BC to 1200BC) onwards.

During the Roman occupation (43AD to 410AD) larger settlements were established; the most significant Roman remains visible in Hampshire today are at Portchester Castle in the Portsmouth conurbation; *Calleva*, a former town near the village of Silchester in Basingstoke and Deane; and a large villa at Rockbourne in the New Forest. Fragments of Roman pottery can still be found in the New Forest, particularly in the area of Amberwood Inclosure.

Once the Romans departed, the region was incorporated into the Anglo-Saxon kingdom of Wessex which, after defeating neighbouring Mercia in 825AD, became the most dominant kingdom in southern England. The Wessex royal court was based in Winchester, although it spent most of its time touring its domains – a common practice of royal courts of the era. Prior to the end of the 12th century, Winchester was the most important city in England and was Wessex's de facto capital. Hampshire's role as an administrative unit within the kingdom can be traced back to the 8th century.

In 1015 the Danish prince Cnut gained control of Wessex and was crowned King of England two years later. He was buried in 1035 at the Anglo-Saxon cathedral of Old Minster in Winchester, under the site of the current Winchester Cathedral. In 1066 Norman invaders wiped Wessex off the map when they subjugated England. However, the ancient administrative unit of Hampshire has survived to this day and is one of England's wealthiest counties.

The county is named after the

settlement that eventually became the city of Southampton whose population overtook that of Winchester in the 16th century. Southampton was known in Old English as *Hamtun*, meaning 'a small settlement', and its surrounding area, or *scire*, became known as *Hamtunscire*.

The New Forest National Park

The New Forest is imbued with a sense of wilderness and has been the inspiration for artists, poets and writers since a nascent tourism industry arose in the 18th century. The park covers 566 sq km and its survival as the largest contiguous area of unfenced pasture, heath and forest in lowland Britain is due to its poor acidic soils which are unsuited to agriculture.

Having defeated the Anglo Saxons, the new Norman rulers turned the region into a royal hunting forest in 1079. The Normans managed hunting forests primarily to provide entertainment in the form of deer and boar hunting, as well as a reliable source of meat for the royal and ecclesiastical elite. Commoners were denied the right to graze their animals in most of the forest and were not allowed to fence their properties, because a fence interfered with the free-running deer and boar. They were only permitted to graze their animals in the so-called 'Open Forest' (areas with few trees). The basis of this system is still in existence today and is administered by the Verderers in Lyndhurst, who play a major role in the management of the national park. The Crown still owns most of the land (around 27,000 hectares) within the park.

Large areas of the New Forest were planted with oak in the 18th century to meet the massive demand for timber for shipbuilding as Britain expanded its global empire and its naval capacity. Many of the inclosures – fenced areas that restrict grazing animals from entering – date from this period. However, the felling of large areas of broadleaved trees began during the First World War to meet the wartime demand for timber. Further felling took place during the Second World War and many such areas were subsequently replanted with conifer species. The focus of the woodland management within the park has shifted away from commercial timber production in more recent years and some conifer plantations within the park's boundaries are being returned to heathland or broadleaved woodland.

Some of the best-known features of the New Forest are the free-roaming horses, ponies, donkeys and cattle on the open heath and in much of the woodland. They can also be spotted mooching about in villages within the park, and often try to enter gardens, homes and shops. Do not feed the horses, as this will encourage scavenging behaviour. Be warned – most of the campsites within the park are unfenced and it is not unusual for a horse to rip open a tent if it smells food inside.

Due to the lack of ploughing over the centuries, numerous Bronze Age round barrows (burial mounds) can still be seen here. There are about 250 round barrows within the park's boundaries, and about 150 scheduled ancient monuments. The New Forest became a national park in 2005.

The South Downs National Park

The South Downs National Park covers an area of 1627 sq km and was established in 2011. Within its boundaries are the counties of Hampshire, West Sussex and East Sussex while the western end of the park is near Winchester. The grassy downlands within the park exhibit some of the rarest floral habitats in England – the result of centuries of grazing and calcareous soils. However, since the Second World War most of these grasslands have been lost to agriculture and what remains is a national treasure. Some of the walks in this guide explore these grasslands, where you are likely to be accompanied in summer by the trill of skylarks overhead and by a variety of butterflies and other insects.

Wildlife

Specialist heathland birds are widespread in the New Forest and the woodlands support a variety of bird species, some of which are nationally rare. The grasslands of the South Downs provide a habitat for a variety of birds, some of which are nationally rare. All three British native species of snake inhabit the New Forest.

Throughout Hampshire, you can see deer. Fallow deer are the most common, having been introduced by the Normans. To see them up close, head to the viewing platform at Bolderwood Deer Sanctuary in the New Forest, where there are daily feeding sessions in summer.

European otter can be found along some watercourses and, thanks to conservation efforts, the European polecat – once persecuted to extinction in England – has in recent years recolonised former territory in western Hampshire.

About this guide

Hampshire is well connected with other regions by bus and train; many routes in this guide depart from villages and can be reached by bus. Public transport and parking availability is indicated in each route introduction. Most walks are circular and all return to the point of departure.

Although these routes are generally moderate, a few do include steep gradients and this is also highlighted in the route introduction. Walk times are calculated as the average time taken by a moderately fit walker and should be used as a rough guide only. The sketch maps in this guide are for illustrative purposes only and it is recommended that you carry the relevant OS map which shows the landscape in more detail, including the rights of way. This is especially useful if you want to modify or extend your walk.

Viewed from above, the New Forest appears as a deep green nucleus set within a jumbled patchwork of multi-hued fields. Its woodlands and heaths resound with birdsong, while early summer breezes carry the scent of gorse flowers. In winter the bare branches of gnarled oaks cloaked by valley fogs create scenes of startling beauty. It is remarkable that such a sanctuary exists in the densely populated south of England. Around 16 million people live within a 90-minute drive of the New Forest, yet the park's open, unfenced expanse provides an approximation of wilderness that is unparalleled in southern England.

Most of the walks in this chapter are within the park's boundaries, although also included here is the coast at Keyhaven Marshes Nature Reserve, a great spot for birdwatchers in winter, and Rockbourne, arguably the prettiest village in Hampshire and the site of a painstakingly excavated Roman villa. During summer the car parks of the New Forest can be busy, particularly at weekends. Despite this, you don't have to walk far to escape the crowds.

Keep your eyes peeled for veteran oaks; the oldest trees were once coppiced or pollarded, a practice which became illegal in the New Forest in 1698 in order to increase the yield of large-diameter logs for shipbuilding. Multiple boughs sprouting from a short but unusually thick trunk are a sure sign that an oak has been pollarded.

The New Forest

Rockbourne

Distance 13km **Time** 4 hours
Terrain grassy lanes and estate tracks,
woodland track; mostly easy walking
with some gentle hills **Map** OS Explorer
OL22 **Access** buses from Fordingbridge;
if you intend to visit the Rose and Thistle
you may park in the pub car park at the
landlord's discretion (check opening
times before you set out), otherwise
there is very limited on-street parking

Rockbourne is one of Hampshire's most
stunning villages. This walk, starting and
ending at the village pub, takes in an
impressive estate where you may see
racehorses on the gallops amidst
glorious rolling hills. After your walk you
could peruse the excavated Roman villa
south of Rockbourne.

From the Rose and Thistle pub, turn
right along the main village street and
then left at a sign for Manor Farm
directing you along a lane. Continue
straight ahead opposite some farm
buildings to join a bridleway heading
uphill as a grassy track through a field
studded with veteran oaks.

At the top of the field, continue through
two metal gates to enter a woodland strip
dominated by mature beech. Pass
through a series of gates to enter a wide
grassy avenue flanked by large trees. Go
through the white gate at the top of the
avenue and, shortly after this, turn right
onto the road before turning left onto a
footpath next to the entrance to The
Manor. The route follows an asphalt track.

Just beyond the pretty thatched barns,
follow a bridleway waymarker along a
surfaced track. When this swings to the
left, continue straight ahead on a grassy
track heading downhill between fields.

At a T-junction at the bottom of the hill,
turn left for an easy 2km on the wide
grassy Long Steeple Lane. At the
crossroads of lanes just after a metal gate,

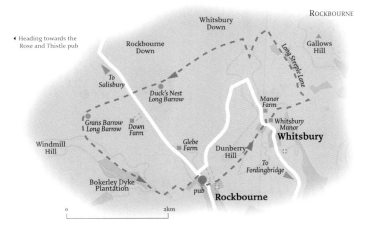

◄ Heading towards the Rose and Thistle pub

bear left to head uphill on a gravel track flanked by wooden fences.

Reaching a three-pronged waymarker near the top of the hill, bear sharp right and descend towards a strip of trees. At a junction of lanes just below the trees, bear left and, in around 300m, continue straight ahead through a crossroads of lanes. This grassy lane leads you for another 2km or so to emerge at the public road at the entrance to Tenantry Farm.

Cross the road and continue straight ahead for about 1km. Just after passing a pylon on the hilltop, go left through a gate to follow the left-hand field margin. Near the top left corner of the field, go left through a gap in the hedge and continue uphill on the field margin with a hedge on your right.

At the corner of the field, go through a gap in the hedge to join a track, where you turn right. Pass through the gate just ahead and turn left. When you meet

woodland at the corner of the field, go through the metal gate. The path may be a bit overgrown as it enters the woodland, but improves a short distance ahead.

After about 300m, turn right at the junction of paths to follow a yellow waymarker arrow and go through a gate. Continue adjacent to the wire fence. The undulations in the ground, clearly visible in the woods at Bokerley Dyke Plantation, are the remains of an Iron Age fort.

Once you've left the woodland, ignore the yellow waymarker arrow at a kissing gate and continue straight on, keeping the hedge on your right-hand side. Turn left at a waymarker (a trig point is visible in the adjacent field) to head steeply uphill to a ridge and down the other side. Follow the waymarker arrow after reaching the bottom of the field; the path soon joins a grassy lane which leads to the main street in Rockbourne. Turn right here to return to the Rose and Thistle.

Blashford Lakes

Distance 4km **Time** 1 hour
Terrain level, well-made surfaced paths
Map OS Explorer OL22; a downloadable
map of the reserve is available from
Hampshire and Isle of Wight Wildlife
Trust website **Access** no public transport
to the start; car park at Tern Hide (open
until 16:30) to the north of Ellingham
Drove, or National Trust Rockford
Common car park east of the walk

Blashford Lakes Nature Reserve, a series
of former gravel extraction pits, is one
of the best places in England to see
overwintering birds. The reserve
includes seven bird hides linked by
surfaced paths. Please note, dogs are
not allowed in most of the reserve itself
but by parking at Rockford Common
you may follow the main loop, keeping
dogs on a lead between Ivy and
Rockford Lakes.

Surveys have estimated that up to 5000
birds visit Blashford Lakes during the
winter, a time of year when numbers are
boosted due to the annual migration.
Visiting in summer is still recommended,
however, and you are guaranteed
sightings of several feathered species.
Common terns, lapwings and
oystercatchers are often seen feeding on
the lakes, and there is an abundance of
dragonflies and damselflies.

From the car park at Tern Hide, follow
the path that runs parallel to the car park
access road. Cross Ellingham Drove and
after a short distance bear left at a fork to
cross a footbridge. Turn left after crossing
the bridge to follow the path alongside
the Dockens Water – one of the cleanest
river systems in Europe. Shortly after this,
you pass another footbridge and path on
the left signposted for the Lapwing and
Goosander Hides. Continue eastwards on
the south side of the Dockens Water,
following the signpost for the Alice Lisle
pub. Benches along the path make good
rest stops to enjoy the woodland. The
path becomes less well-maintained when
it exits the reserve.

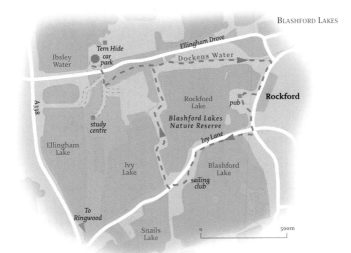

Tern Hide
car park
Ibsley Water
Ellingham Drove
Dockens Water
A338
study centre
Rockford Lake
pub
Rockford
Blashford Lakes Nature Reserve
Ellingham Lake
Ivy Lane
Ivy Lake
Blashford Lake
sailing club
To Ringwood
Snails Lake
0   500m

After leaving the woodland, the path continues adjacent to a fence below powerlines for just over 500m, with views of Rockford Lake to your right. Follow the path as it swings 90° to the right at the field corner. After 200m or so, go through a gate and turn right to head towards the Alice Lisle pub in the hamlet of Rockford.

Alice Lisle was an aristocrat born in 1617 at nearby Ellingham whose fortunes changed in 1685 when she was charged with harbouring fugitives after the defeat of the Monmouth Rebellion (an attempt to overthrow King James II) at the Battle of Sedgemoor in Somerset. The unfortunate Alice was the last woman to be sentenced to execution by beheading by an English court. The presiding Judge Jeffreys was a servile royalist known to be a severe enforcer of punishment.

After a refreshing drink and possibly lunch, continue past the pub car park and go through a pedestrian gate next to a cattle grid. In around 100m, just after passing both Ivy Lane and the entrance to Ivy Cottage, turn right to go through a gate to a footpath. This is part of the Avon Valley long-distance path. The path wanders through clouds of honeysuckle in summer as it makes its way between Ivy Lane and the shore of Blashford Lake.

A few metres after passing the entrance to Spinnaker Sailing Club, cross Ivy Lane and go through a kissing gate to re-enter Blashford Lakes Nature Reserve. The route continues along a woodland strip for about 800m with views across Ivy Lake to your left and Rockford Lake to your right, passing some bird hides. At a T-junction of paths, bear left to retrace your steps to the car park at the start.

◀ Preening common tern at Blashford Lakes

Frogham

Distance 8km **Time** 2 hours 30
Terrain wide gravel paths and woodland
tracks; gently undulating hills
Map OS Explorer OL22 **Access** buses from
Fordingbridge to nearby Ogdens and
Hyde; car parks at Ogdens and Frogham

This scenic circuit features dramatic
undulating moorland and a woodland
of mature Scots pine and Douglas fir
whose resinous scent on a summer's
breeze is a delight. Another woodland
along the way includes both broadleaves
and mixed conifers and is a haven for a
variety of birds and deer.

A large car park at Frogham marks
the start of this walk. Near the southern
end of the car park, almost opposite a

pond fed by a spring, is an information
panel with details about this Site of
Special Scientific Interest (SSSI) and
Special Protected Area (SPA). Take the
track next to the information panel
which soon starts to descend.

On meeting a wider gravel track in just
over 100m, bear left to head towards a
minor road. Turn right onto the broad
track just before the road. Clumps of
gorse, bracken and grass abound here,
with bog cotton marking marshy areas
near the track which climbs gently on a
ridge, providing some great views.

Soon after passing a clump of
broadleaves, and just before the track
veers to the left, bear right onto a less
well-used track. Aim for the conifer

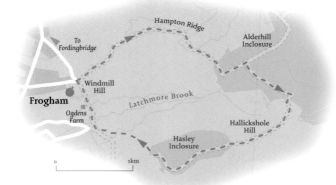

plantation (Alderhill Inclosure) visible ahead. The track drops downhill and enters the plantation.

At a junction of paths soon after entering the plantation, turn left. At another junction about 350m ahead, turn right to walk down a gravel track leading over a footbridge and through a couple of gates that flank a glade containing a corral. Beyond the gates the track starts to ascend gently. Continue straight ahead, ignoring any trails that peel off from it.

Keep your eye out for a track on your right leading out of the woodland via a gate after 500m. Once through this gate, the track levels out and you are again treated to sweeping views. Carry on along this track to reach a broadleaf and mixed conifer woodland (Hasley Inclosure) about 1km ahead.

After entering the woodland via a gate, continue straight ahead, ignoring the path to the right just after the gate. Pass straight through a couple of crossroads

before turning left at a T-junction of paths. A few metres ahead, go through a gate to leave the woodland on a path that is fairly indistinct. Look for a stand of Scots pines and bear right to join a gravel track beyond this.

The track soon splits to become several faint paths. Take the one that is the most well-used, bearing slightly to the left across a flat grassy area for about 850m. When you reach an unsurfaced minor road and a couple of cottages, bear right. Just ahead is a sign for Ogdens car park.

Continue through the car park and follow the track beyond the vehicle barrier. This track passes the entrance to Ogdens Farm and climbs uphill beside a deer fence. At the brow of the hill, about 350m beyond the entrance to Ogdens Farm, take the track to the left, passing a line of posts embedded in the ground, which returns you to the car park at Frogham.

◀ Moorland trail at Frogham

Vales Moor

Distance 2km **Time** 45 minutes
Terrain gravel and sandy tracks across
gently undulating heathland
Map OS Explorer OL22 **Access** no public
transport to the start; car park at the
start of the walk

This short stroll includes a section of
the Smugglers' Road, which was used
during the 18th and early 19th centuries
to transport contraband from the coast.
Smuggling, or 'free-trading', was
common in the region due to high taxes,
and Burley was once an important hub
of this trade.

Contraband included brandy, tobacco,
tea and lace, which were subject to the
highest taxes. Customs men tended to
avoid confronting the citizens of Burley,
who were able to raise an armed troop
of men at short notice and were more

than a match for the king's officers.

Local folklore claims that Burley
Beacon, a hill just outside Burley, was the
site of a dragon's lair. The dragon was
apparently slain by the brave Sir Maurice
Berkeley, lord of the nearby Bisterne
manor, and the site of the Battle of
Bisterne is still called 'Dragon Fields'.
Several pubs in the vicinity have been
named the 'Green Dragon' over the years
to commemorate this beast.

From the car park named Smugglers'
Road, located on the road between Burley
Street and Crow, head past the
information panel onto the wide eroded
path heading gently uphill. After passing
a clump of gorse bushes, turn left onto
the path leading uphill towards more
gorse bushes and young birch trees.

At the brow of the hill, join the wide
track (Smugglers' Road) and turn right.

◄ View from the Smugglers' Road

The Smugglers' Road continues along a ridge and is almost level, with panoramic views across heather-clad hills dotted with mature broadleaves and woodlands. Combined with the gently undulating hills, the overall effect is a visual oxymoron of unintended landscaping and orderly ruggedness.

Leave the Smugglers' Road at the third path leading off to the right, around 450m after joining the route. The path is quite narrow and easy to miss, so keep your eyes peeled. After leaving the Smugglers' Road you descend the hill and turn right to join the path heading gently downhill along the bottom of the valley. Follow the most well-used route in the valley floor, which leads towards the public road that links Burley Street and Crow. The few lonely pines along the valley, combined with the heather moorland, create a scene redolent of alpine regions.

After passing straight through a couple of path intersections, you arrive back at the Smugglers' Road car park.

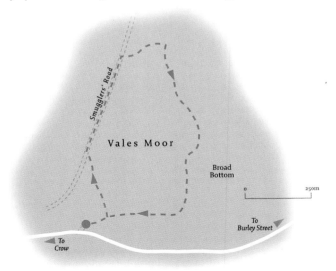

Bolderwood Deer Sanctuary

Distance 3km **Time** 1 hour
Terrain wide mostly level forest trails
Map OS Explorer OL22 **Access** no public
transport to the start; car park at the
start of the walk

The herd of fallow deer at Bolderwood
Deer Sanctuary leads a charmed life.
Between April and September, they are
fed daily from 12:30 to 14:30 at a viewing
platform by a ranger. Watching them
close up while they munch contentedly
has become a popular attraction and if
you are here in October, you might get a
good view of the deer rutting.

Bolderwood Deer Sanctuary is about
6km west of Lyndhurst and is signposted
from the road only as 'Bolderwood'. The
sanctuary includes an arboretum with
some fine specimens from around the
world, and there is a picnic area near the

car park which includes installations
for disposable barbecues.

From the information panel in the car
park, head into the woodland on the
Radnor Trail, waymarked with wooden
posts topped with red. The route wends
through woodland which wouldn't look
out of place in British Columbia, with
western red cedar, Douglas fir and western
hemlock naturally regenerating and
surrounded by their offspring. The
woodland is filled with their resinous
scent on a warm summer's day. There
are also some broadleaved species
(native to Britain) and wooden benches
placed thoughtfully along the route to
enable you to sit and enjoy the
woodland ambience.

The Forestry Commission are doing a
good job of managing this forest for
wildlife and amenity purposes and it

◀ Woodland at Bolderwood Deer Sanctuary

is a real delight to walk through. The silvicultural system applied here is known as 'continuous cover'. This system mimics natural forest dynamics and only single trees, or small groups of trees, are removed once they reach a certain size so that natural regeneration can take place. This system is rarely economically viable when compared with clear-felling and demands more input from forest managers, which is why it is little practised in Britain. It is becoming more common, however, in some of the Forestry Commission's most popular woodlands, as it is deemed to be more attractive than clear felling and of more benefit to wildlife. The continuous cover system is harder to implement with broadleaf species due to grazing pressure from deer,

which have a penchant for eating most broadleaves.

A short way into the woods, just past a plaque commemorating the planting of the woodland in 1969 on the 50th anniversary of the Forestry Commission, you can bear right on a path to visit the deer viewing platform or leave that until the end of the walk. Otherwise, continue following the easy-to-spot waymarkers forming the Radnor Trail to complete this pleasant circuit.

Lyndhurst

**Distance 6.5km Time 2 hours
Terrain gently undulating graded forest
tracks and well-used woodland trails
Map OS Explorer OL22 Access buses from
Lymington and Southampton stop at
Clayhill; car park at the start of the walk**

**This easy, relatively flat walk takes you
on forest tracks through stunning
broadleaf and mixed conifer woodland,
and through several inclosures, which
have been a management feature of the
New Forest since medieval times and still
provide high-quality timber. The rich
habitat ensures that you will see a range
of butterflies and birds in summer.**

Clayhill was once home to Brusher
Mills, an eccentric hermit who made a
living catching adders and grass snakes
to sell to tourists and London Zoo back in
the late 1800s. It is estimated that during
his career Mills caught more than 30,000

of these creatures, no doubt decimating
local populations. He is commemorated
by a pub named The Snakecatcher in
nearby Brockenhurst.

A car park on the eastern edge of
Clayhill, a hamlet around 1km south of
the centre of Lyndhurst, marks the start
of this walk. To get to the car park, turn
off the A337 at Beechen Lane, about 300m
north of the Crown Stirrup pub. The car
park is at the end of Beechen Lane.

From here, head through the gates
leading onto a wide forest track and
continue for about 1.5km to marker post
270 (part of a waymarked mountain biking
circuit). The enclosed woodland
compartments abound with yew, hazel
and oak, as well as dense naturally-
regenerating undergrowth – a result of
the exclusion of deer and horses. The
trackside verges punctuated with piles of
decaying logs provide a fantastic insect

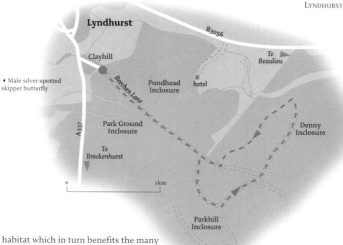

Lyndhurst

B3056

Clayhill

To Beaulieu

◀ Male silver-spotted skipper butterfly

Beechen Lane

Pondhead Inclosure

hotel

Park Ground Inclosure

Denny Inclosure

A337

To Brockenhurst

0   1km

Parkhill Inclosure

habitat which in turn benefits the many birds. You may see song thrushes here, a species that has declined dramatically in most of England and is red listed as a bird of serious conservation concern.

At waymarker post 270, turn right to go through a gate to a track heading slightly downhill. This track intersects mixed conifer and broadleaf woodland, with some grand specimens of Douglas fir. The forest is managed for commercial timber production and the compartments of trees of differing age classes provide a valuable habitat for a variety of critters.

When you reach a junction of paths marked by waymarker post 271, bear left to head uphill and past waymarker post 283, then go through a gate leading into Parkhill Inclosure where an open heather-dominated glade bears away to your right with woodland on your left. Continue straight ahead on the track through the

inclosure for just over 600m, then go through a gate to carry on directly ahead into Denny Inclosure. After just over 350m, you come to a gate which marks the northern boundary of Denny Inclosure.

Immediately after you have exited Denny Inclosure, turn left onto a less well-used path accompanied by a fence. Follow the fence to a gate and a crossroads of paths, where you continue straight ahead to a T-junction.

At the T-junction, turn right before going left after a short distance. This track leads you through a gate and gently uphill to arrive at waymarker post 280 next to a magnificent oak after about 400m. Turn right here to join the forest track leading to the car park (Beechen Lane) and perhaps a refreshing drink at the Crown Stirrup.

19

Brockenhurst

**Distance 8.5km Time 2 hours 30
Terrain** gently undulating woodland
paths and minor roads **Map** OS Explorer
OL22 **Access** buses from Salisbury,
Lymington, Ringwood, Lyndhurst,
Beaulieu and Burley; trains from London
Waterloo, Weymouth and Lymington;
parking at St Nicholas' Church at
the start

This picturesque outing takes you from
the medieval St Nicholas' Parish Church
and through the delightful Roydon
Woods Nature Reserve. The church's
unusual stained-glass windows depict
the First World War field hospital which
once stood nearby and which treated
hundreds of wounded New Zealand
soldiers (the churchyard contains
Commonwealth war graves). This circuit
also visits Boldre Church, once a centre
of clandestine smuggling activity.

St Nicholas' Church is of Norman
origin but sits on a pre-Christian religious
site; the yew in the churchyard has been
accurately dated from core samples to be
more than 1000 years old.

From the church, head south on
Church Lane and bear left at the bridleway
waymarker just after the lane swings to
the right. It's worth pausing for a moment
to admire the classic estate parkland
belonging to Brockenhurst Park, before
continuing past a sign announcing the
entrance to Roydon Woods Nature
Reserve. The reserve contains some fine
gnarled oaks and an abundance of holly,
which forms an overarching canopy at
times. Follow the path as it wends its
way through the reserve until you come
to a junction of three tracks and a
fingerpost after around 1.5km. Here, you
keep going downhill, passing a brick
cottage (Roydon Lodge).

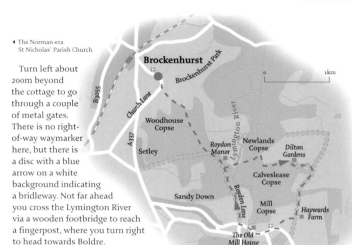

◀ The Norman-era
St Nicholas' Parish Church

Brockenhurst

Brockenhurst Park

B3055

Church Lane

A337

Woodhouse
Copse

Setley

Roydon
Manor

Lymington River

Newlands
Copse

Dilton
Gardens

Calveslease
Copse

Sandy Down

Roydon Lane

Mill
Copse

Haywards
Farm

The Old
Mill House

0   1km

Turn left about 200m beyond the cottage to go through a couple of metal gates. There is no right-of-way waymarker here, but there is a disc with a blue arrow on a white background indicating a bridleway. Not far ahead you cross the Lymington River via a wooden footbridge to reach a fingerpost, where you turn right to head towards Boldre.

After about 800m you emerge from the woodland at the entrance to Dilton Gardens. Continue straight ahead here, and in about 200m turn right at the T-junction onto an unsurfaced track and carry on for another 800m to Haywards Farm. Turn right onto the path adjacent to a thatched cottage opposite the farmhouse. A waymarker indicates the route here.

In 300m or so, you join a minor road at Boldre Church, dedicated to St John. The church dates to 1087 and, in addition to providing spiritual nourishment for the pious, it was a clandestine store for smugglers' contraband during the 'golden era' of smuggling in southern England in the 18th and early 19th centuries. The church was well-placed for use in this illicit trade, being on a crossroads and not far from the Lymington River. Many locals sympathised with the smugglers, due to the exorbitant taxes levied on imports from abroad, as well as the extreme poverty of most of the rural population.

Carry straight on along the road, ignoring other roads branching off to the left. On reaching a crossroads, turn right to head along a signposted 'no-through road', at the end of which continue straight ahead onto the unsurfaced track to re-enter Roydon Woods Nature Reserve and return to Roydon Lodge. From here, retrace your outward journey, keeping in mind that you should bear right at the fingerpost a short distance uphill beyond Roydon Lodge.

Langley

Distance 7km **Time** 2 hours
Terrain almost level tracks between
fields, across a common and through
woodland **Map** OS Explorer OL22
Access buses from Southampton, Hythe,
Lepe and Calshot; limited on-street
parking near the start of the walk

This tour starts just south of Langley
Tavern and takes you across an attractive
common and along tracks between
fields. The twin chimneys of the nearby
Fawley Refinery rise like incongruous
Titans above the common, lending the
scene a somewhat surreal aspect.

  Head south from Langley Tavern for
about 50m and cross the road to continue
along a footpath next to Seaview Cottage.
The path skirts the cottage's garden and
continues between fields. Turn left on
arriving at a path junction next to a
pylon and pass between two hedges
to continue along the field edge with
a hedge on your right.

  After passing an electric substation, go
through a kissing gate to a junction of
paths and turn left, ignoring the entrance
to Mopley Farm. At the junction of
Mopley and Green Lane, turn right to
follow Green Lane, which is lined on the
left with houses.

  Turn right where Green Lane meets
Walkers Lane South to go through a gate
giving access to Fields Heath and Tom's
Down. Bear left at the path junction just
after the gate, ignoring another gate on
your left a little further ahead. Follow
the wide gravel path through a landscape of
copses, gorse and open areas for around
650m. Avoid taking any narrower paths
leading off the main route.

  At a T-junction, bear left, then
immediately right. The twin chimneys of
Fawley Refinery are visible on your left,

◄ Old oaks at Langley

beyond the open ground dotted with shrubs. On arriving at a pylon about 300m ahead, turn right and follow the path bounded by a wire fence.

About 175m after passing the pylon, go through a gateway with a missing gate and bear right, ignoring the path to the left with overarching branches. Keep following the path that runs adjacent to a barbed-wire fence and beneath powerlines, ignoring paths that lead off from it. A short distance ahead, the wire fence swings to the right. Don't follow it but carry on along the path accompanied by the powerlines.

Continue straight ahead through a crossroads of paths. You stop following the powerlines here. At a junction about 300m or so ahead, take the middle path that crosses a woodland plantation and goes through the gate ahead.

After crossing a stream via a footbridge, continue straight ahead and exit the woods into open farmland. About 250m after the footbridge, turn right at the junction of paths next to some houses. In 200m, go through the gate and continue straight ahead, ignoring the path peeling off to your right.

In just over 1km, turn left to go through the kissing gate you passed earlier near the electric transformer station and follow the path back to the start point.

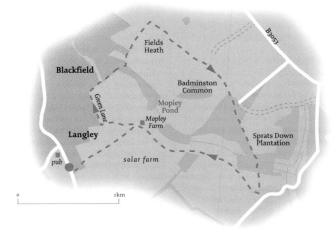

Keyhaven Marshes

Distance **8km** Time **2 hours**
Terrain **level well-made graded paths**
Map **OS Explorer OL22** Access **buses from Brockenhurst and Lymington; car park and parking bays at the start of the walk**

This pleasant excursion around Keyhaven Marshes Nature Reserve takes you along the coast and around brackish lagoons where you can enjoy the sight of a variety of seabirds feeding, chattering and preening. The reserve is a mosaic of ponds and water-filled ditches amidst marshes grazed by cattle.

The marshes have a long history as salterns: salt was harvested here from Roman times until 1865 when the lagoons were converted into oyster beds. To create the salt, seawater was impounded in these shallow lagoons and left to evaporate. The brine solution was drawn off with windpumps and transferred to large metal pans where it was heated until only the salt remained. Sailing barges would dock to import coal and export the salt. Moses Dock, which is about halfway along this walk, is the only remaining navigable dock.

The salinity of the water within the lagoons, which are connected by sluices, is generally lower than seawater, creating the perfect conditions for a variety of seashore plants, such as thrift, samphire and sea campion. It is also an important habitat for birds such as ringed plover, black-tailed godwit, shelduck, avocet, curlew, lapwing and wigeon.

From Keyhaven Road, follow the dead-end road opposite Hawkers Cottage and alongside the north side of Keyhaven

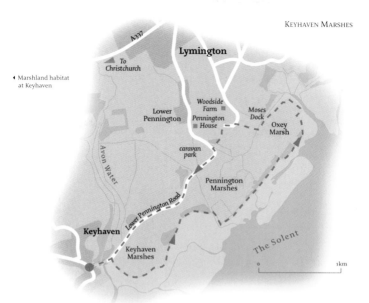

◄ Marshland habitat
at Keyhaven

Amenity Car Park. Turn right after a series of parking bays to take the path through the gate and along the seawall for 4.5km. The Isle of Wight is clearly visible 3km across The Solent.

Continue along the coastal path until you meet a footbridge over sluice gates at Moses Dock. Instead of crossing the footbridge, turn left to descend a few steps and carry on along a path next to the canal.

Ignore the path that swings to the right to follow the canal bank 150m beyond Moses Dock, and instead continue on the wide path straight ahead. After a further 150m, you arrive at a T-junction where you turn right to go through a gate.

In about 250m, go through another gate and turn left onto a road. The road ends after passing a couple of houses a further 250m ahead, and you continue straight on along a footpath flanked by trees.

Where you meet another road, turn left and follow this until it meets a gravel track after about 400m. Take this track and ignore paths peeling off from it a few metres ahead. You will pass Hurst View camping and caravan site and a small lagoon in a field where you may see Brent geese, depending on the season.

After about 1.5km you meet a road. Continue straight ahead to reach the car park and the end of the walk.

Beaulieu and Buckler's Hard

Distance 7.5km Time 2 hours
Terrain level graded paths and
unsurfaced paths Map OS Explorer OL22
Access buses from Brockenhurst, Hythe,
Lyndhurst and Lymington; car parks at
Beaulieu and Buckler's Hard

This classic New Forest adventure starts
at the Montagu Arms Hotel, named after
the family who have owned the Beaulieu
Estate since the 16th century. Take time
to explore Beaulieu's charming streets
and shops before heading to Buckler's
Hard, a former shipyard replete with
lawns, harbourside café and cosy pub.

From the Montagu Arms in Beaulieu,
follow the sign for the Solent Way, a long-
distance footpath. The route skirts the
hotel car park via Fire Station Lane, which
becomes a gravel track just beyond the
fire station.

After going through a gate, follow the
waymarked route towards Buckler's

Hard, arriving at a few buildings named
Bailey's Hard in about 1km. Brick
manufacturing at Bailey's Hard
commenced in 1790 and ceased in 1935.
The kiln has since been restored.
Navigable from the sea, the site was also
chosen for the availability of clay to make
the bricks. Peak production took place
with the expansion of the railway system
in the late 1840s, when the bricks could be
transported to a much wider area,
including the towns of Bournemouth,
Southampton and further afield.

Around 100m after Bailey's Hard, bear
left on the riverside walk to Buckler's
Hard. This route can be muddy in winter
but is more scenic than the straight
march (on the albeit better path) without
views along the Solent Way – which you'll
be following on the return from Buckler's
Hard. The walk wends along the banks of
the Beaulieu River from here and
provides pleasant views of saltmarshes

and yachts on their moorings.

After 1.5km the riverside path rejoins the Solent Way. A path to the left here leads to Keeping Marsh bird hide. Continue to Buckler's Hard, passing Agamemnon Boat Yard. *HMS Agamemnon* was built here and launched in 1781 during the American War of Independence before being recommissioned at the start of the French Revolutionary War (1793) under Captain Nelson. Said to be Nelson's favourite ship, it was affectionately renamed 'Eggs and Bacon' by the crew – the classical names much in vogue among the elite (Agamemnon was the king of Mycenae in Greek mythology) did not strike a chord with the men who crewed the ships.

Follow the signposted track for the Maritime Museum and Master Builder's Hotel. A little further ahead is the Duke's Bath House, a quaint building that was originally constructed by Lord Montagu as a bathhouse for his son, who had arthritis. It was believed at the time that taking baths in saline water would alleviate this and other conditions. The building later became accommodation for estate labourers.

The path terminates at the Master Builder's Hotel at the bottom end of two rows of attractive buildings facing each other across a wide lawn. The remains of

six ship-launching ramps are visible at the riverside. This peaceful spot was once a hive of activity where a number of warships were created for Nelson's fleet. In the 1720s the harbour was envisaged to be the start of 'Montagu Town', which would refine lucrative sugar cane from the West Indies. However, the plan failed when an expedition funded by the second Duke to take control of the island of St Lucia was thwarted by the French.

At the top of the rows of houses is the Maritime Museum. After perusing the sights at Buckler's Hard, head back the way you came as far as the Keeping Marsh junction, then return along the Solent Way. At Beaulieu you could continue the historic theme by visiting the remains of a partially ruined Cistercian Abbey, founded in 1204.

◄ Yachts on the Beaulieu River

Male banded demoiselle damselfly ▶

of year, a refreshing drink or meal is a perfect way to round off a walk.

The district is named after the River Test, which originates near Ashe in Basingstoke & Deane and enters the sea at Southampton. It is one of the world's most popular fly-fishing rivers, its crystal-clear waters a result of the chalk substrate. This porous calcareous rock acts like an immense filtration system for rainwater which, once it hits an impervious layer, collects in huge aquifers, seeping out as springs that feed the Hampshire river systems with beautifully clear water.

The Test Valley is also known for its horse racing and training. The first walk in this chapter, at Wildhern, takes you alongside a training track, known as a gallop. The chalky soil of the Test Valley and other northern regions of the county makes good-quality turf suitable for the impact of horses' hooves.

The terrain of this region is gently undulating, which lends itself to easy walking, as well as making the panoramic views from Danebury Hill Fort all the more impressive. Some sections of the walks follow ancient lanes. Lane-side earthworks, often concealed by trees, indicate that the route was once a drove road, where the banked sides kept driven animals from wandering. Prior to the advent of railways, droving was carried out on a large scale: drovers had to be over the age of 30, male, married and in possession of a permit.

The Test Valley is notable for its chocolate-box villages where centuries-old timber-framed thatched cottages line the streets, most of them nestled in well-tended gardens. Many of these villages have pubs at their centre, often with beer gardens for basking in during the summer and wood-burning stoves and open fires during the winter. At any time

The Test Valley

Wildhern

Distance 4km **Time** 1 hour **Terrain** mostly flat farmland, unsurfaced lanes and field-side paths **Map** OS Explorer 131 **Access** buses from Andover and Vernham Dean; parking is available at Tangley Village Hall in Wildhern – do not park on the verge if the car park is full; there is no on-street parking in the village

From the small and tranquil village of Wildhern, notable for its neat hedges and gardens, this short stroll takes in some classic Hampshire countryside. The first half of the walk is on the Brenda Parker Way, a long-distance footpath. From Doles Farm an unsurfaced lane and field-side paths bring you back to Wildhern.

Starting at Wildhern's village hall, which is on the road towards Hatherden, walk back for around 200m to Wildhern's main street. Cross this and take the path directly opposite, waymarked as the Brenda Parker Way.

Follow the Brenda Parker Way for just over 1km to Doles Farm. This is wheat and barley country and you will most likely see these crops in the fields as you stroll towards the farm. You may also spot a variety of butterflies along this stretch in warmer months.

Turn right at a metal gate at the entrance to the farm buildings, following a right of way that avoids taking you through the farmyard. Just after passing the farm buildings, turn right at the path junction and go straight ahead at another junction a short distance further on. The route carries on along an unsurfaced lane which takes you through the western fringe of Rag Wood for around 400m.

Continue straight ahead once you have

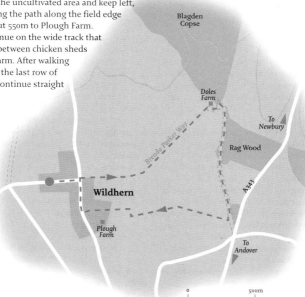

◄ Field-side path at Wildhern

left the wood and, after about 450m, keep your eyes peeled for a gap in the hedge into a field on your right, opposite a small copse: it's waymarked but tends to be overgrown and easy to miss. If you reach the busy A343, you've gone too far.

Follow the left-hand field edge as it heads gently uphill. After about 400m the path arrives at a junction with an uncultivated turning area on your right. Ignore the uncultivated area and keep left, following the path along the field edge for about 550m to Plough Farm.

Continue on the wide track that passes between chicken sheds at the farm. After walking beyond the last row of sheds, continue straight

ahead towards three maple trees. Don't follow the farm track as it swings to the right before the trees; instead just beyond the maples you'll find a right-of-way marker. Follow the path next to this, which passes between garden fences. When in a short while you arrive at Wildhern's main street, turn right and then left onto the road signposted for Hatherden to return to the village hall.

Blagden
Copse

Doles
Farm

To
Newbury

Brenda Parker Way

Rag Wood

A343

Wildhern

Plough
Farm

To
Andover

0   500m

Abbotts Ann

Distance 6km **Time** 1 hour 30
Terrain level paths along field edges
Map OS Explorer 131 **Access** buses from
Andover, Winchester, The Wallops and
Salisbury; on-street parking available
in Abbotts Ann

**This easy stroll takes you along the
edges of large fields. Although there
are no long-distance views, you get the
impression of 'big-sky country' due to
the size of the fields and flatness of the
landscape. The route around the fields
is well waymarked.**

Lying about 3km southwest of Andover,
Abbotts Ann is a pleasant village with a
pub, an award-winning shop staffed by
volunteers, and a church displaying 49
'virgins' crowns' – the making of which is
a custom that harks back to the medieval
period, although the most recent crown in
the collection dates from 1973. In the early

days of Christianity, funeral garlands were
emblems of virgin martyrs and the
practice of making maidens' garlands
presumably derives from that.

The Ann in the village's name is of
Celtic origin, and is derived from *Anne*,
meaning 'wooded banks of a stream'.
There are many such riverside 'Anne'
place names in Britain which share this
etymology. Abbotts Ann sits almost on
the confluence of Pillhill Brook and
the River Anton. As such, the site
undoubtedly has a long history of human
habitation, as in prehistory the waterways
were commonly used for transportation,
with settlements often growing around
river confluences.

From the village pub (The Eagle),
head downhill to the road junction just
past the village shop and post office.
Turn left at the junction to head towards
Monxton, turning immediately left

◀ Cottages at Abbotts Ann

again onto Dunkirt Lane which is waymarked with a fingerpost, pointing you towards Stockbridge.

After passing some attractive houses and gardens Dunkirt Lane ends and a concrete lane continues between fields. Carry straight on along this lane, ignoring the footpaths leading off to the left and right, until you reach a barn after about 1.5km.

Turn left here, as indicated by the waymarker, and follow the field edge with a small woodland (The Groves) on your left. Follow the waymarkers as the path continues skirting the edges of fields, sometimes with 90° turns. When you come to a path T-junction with a woodland (Cossical Copse) stretching to the left immediately in front of you, go left (the right-hand path leads to some large houses and the A343).

After rounding a field corner about 200m beyond the woodland, go through a gap in the hedge to enter another field. In a further 200m the path enters a woodland strip and joins an

unsurfaced track (The Drove). Continue straight ahead, ignoring the track and path leading off to the right and left further on. The Drove emerges on the main street of Abbotts Ann in just over 1km. Turn left to return to the village pub.

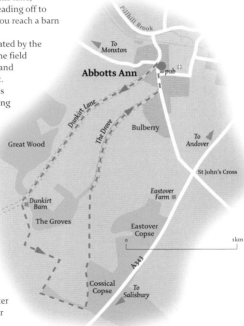

Chilbolton

Distance 4km **Time** 1 hour **Terrain** mostly
waymarked footpaths; path indistinct
across West Down Nature Reserve
Map OS Explorer 131 **Access** buses from
Andover and Stockbridge; car park at the
start and at the southern end of West
Down Nature Reserve, just off the A3057

Chilbolton is a chocolate-box village that
merits a mooch. From a car park near the
main street, head towards the banks of
the River Test, then through West Down
Nature Reserve, before returning to
Chilbolton via footpaths between fields.

The car park at the start of this walk is
at the bottom of Joy's Lane, just off
Chilbolton's main street. Facing the
information panel in the car park, bear
right onto a wide gravel path waymarked
for the Test Way and village playing field.
Beyond the grassy area to your right is
prime otter territory and if you are keen to
spot one of these elusive creatures, it's

best to arrive here at dawn or two hours
before dusk.

Pass a thatched cottage and continue to
the playing field. You can choose to enter
the field at the first gate and then bear
right or continue along the path, entering
the field via a gate further on.
At the eastern end of the playing field, go
through a gate into woodland. The water
meadows just ahead to your right were
created in the 17th and 18th centuries and
were designed to flood regularly, which
ensured plentiful grass for animal fodder.

Cross the road and bear slightly to
the left where an information panel at
the bottom of a lane marks the entrance
to West Down Nature Reserve. The land
here was grazed by sheep until the
Second World War and was devoid of
trees. After the war some of the area was
used for gravel extraction and in the
1960s and 1970s it was a rubbish dump.
Light grazing by cattle is now carried out

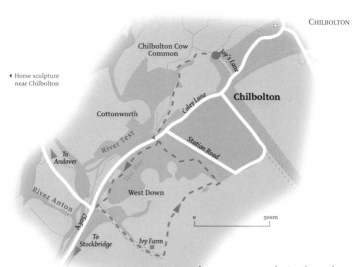

Chilbolton Cow Common

Joy's Lane

Coley Lane

Chilbolton

Cottonworth

Station Road

River Test

To
Andover

Test Way

West Down

River Anton

A3057

To
Stockbridge

Ivy Farm

0   500m

◀ Horse sculpture
near Chilbolton

for conservation purposes to prevent encroachment by scrub and trees.

Bear to the right at the information panel to continue on the Test Way through the reserve. The path is less distinct here. Follow the faint route as it runs parallel to the public road, passing a couple of old iron benches which make good picnic spots along the way.

The route descends to a car park opposite a large house and brick wall on a bend of the A3057. Turn left after exiting the reserve via a gate into the parking area to follow a footpath next to a small brick building. The path leads uphill in a shallow gully bounded by high hedges.

After around 550m the path swings 90° to the left, before soon joining a gravel track at some waterworks. Just beyond a green gate, bear right onto the path into a woodland comprised entirely of hawthorn. Keep following the woodland path and ignore any routes leading off it into fields.

Around 100m or so after entering the hawthorn woodland you come to two parallel paths. Take the left-hand path waymarked as the Test Valley Tour to soon pass an old derelict brick building. Where the path meets a street and houses, turn left to follow the waymarked footpath. After passing the back gardens of some houses, the path enters woodland to emerge at the information panel of the northern entrance to West Down Nature Reserve (which you passed earlier) in around 250m.

From here, retrace your steps to the car park at Chilbolton.

Danebury Hill Fort

Distance 2.5km **Time** 1 hour **Terrain** steep road from the car park and fairly level path around the rim of the fort **Map** OS Explorer 131 **Access** no public transport to the start; two car parks at the fort site

The fort that once crowned Danebury Hill was constructed during the Iron Age, probably in the 6th or 7th century BC, and was occupied for around 500 to 700 years. The site was excavated between 1969 and 1988 and is one of the most studied hillforts in England.

The bodies of about 100 people have been discovered at Danebury, many with injuries consistent with warfare. Other buried remains, of crows and other corvid bird species, suggest ritualistic killings. The massive ditching still evident today indicates the strategic importance of the site, and evidence of an entrance gate burned more than once highlights the precarious existence of its inhabitants during the Iron Age. There are around 2000 Iron Age fort sites in Britain.

From the car park just off the minor road between Stockbridge and Kentsboro, you can head up the steep hill via a public right of way through a couple of fields, or you can walk up the road. If a walk up the steep hill doesn't entice you, there is another car park at the top of the road.

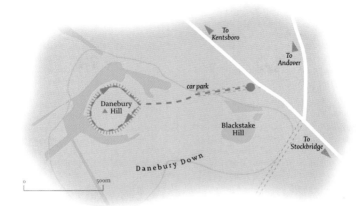

Continue beyond the gate at the top of the road and enter the inner fort site via the former gateway. The path then climbs to the rim of the innermost rampart. You can follow the path around the rim in either direction. There is also a path around the lower rampart, but the higher path provides the best views.

Within the hillfort you may notice that the ground slopes to a high spot in the centre. This area was a focal point for religious gatherings and important meetings. The subtle dips in the ground mark the sites of former grain stores that were unearthed during the excavations. More than 10,000 postholes were also excavated which made up some 500 rectangular buildings along with 73 circular structures believed to have been a mixture of roundhouses and storage buildings. The layout of these suggests they were situated on a central road through the fort that connected the two entrances of the hilltop – the earliest example of a cobbled street in England.

Many hillforts have their origin in the Neolithic period and were often used to contain and protect animals, which were an invaluable source of both milk and meat. Some scholars believe that Danebury was a regional centre of dairy production, due to the unearthing of many items of pottery at the site that once contained milk and the high ratio of female to male cattle bones discovered. There is also evidence of an established trade in iron and salt at Danebury. Some of the artefacts discovered at the site are on display in Andover Museum, which has a section dedicated to the Iron Age.

◀ Iron Age hillfort at Danebury Hill

Ashley

Distance 8km **Time** 2 hours 30
Terrain road walking to start; paths
across and around fields, undulating but
not steep **Maps** OS Explorer 131 and OL32
Access no public transport to the start;
no parking in Ashley; park at Farley
Mount Monument Car Park

**This walk visits a pretty church and
tours an undulating patchwork of fields,
hedges and small woodlands. With wind
rippling the crops and the shrill calls of
a buzzard overhead, this could be the
perfect summertime jaunt.**

As there is no parking in Ashley, the
only option is to start from Farley Mount
Monument Car Park at the west end of
Farley Mount Country Park. From this
car park, bear left on the minor road to
head west for 800m, where you branch

right onto a waymarked bridleway.
This passes through woodland to meet
a driveway giving access to some cottages
and Forest of Bere Farm. Cross the
driveway and continue northwards
with a patch of woodland on your left
and open parkland on your right. After
crossing another asphalt track a few
metres beyond the first, carry on along
a lane (also a bridleway) with hedges
on either side.

The lane continues northwards for 2km,
passing an old pumphouse on the left
along the way, to reach a minor road. Turn
left onto this road to emerge at a three-
way junction with a grassy triangle at the
centre after 250m. Turn left to enter a field
here, as indicated by a waymarker.

Cross the field towards a gap in the
woodland strip visible ahead of you. Walk

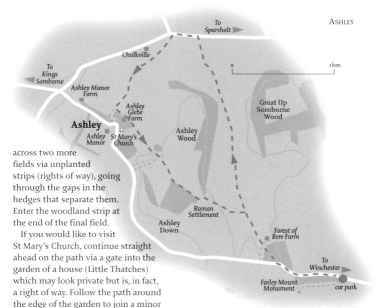

Chalkville

To Sparsholt

To Kings Somborne

Ashley Manor Farm

Ashley Glebe Farm

Ashley

Ashley Manor   *St Mary's Church*

Ashley Wood

Great Up Somborne Wood

Roman Settlement

Ashley Down

Forest of Bere Farm

To Winchester

Farley Mount Monument   *car park*

0   1km

across two more fields via unplanted strips (rights of way), going through the gaps in the hedges that separate them. Enter the woodland strip at the end of the final field.

If you would like to visit St Mary's Church, continue straight ahead on the path via a gate into the garden of a house (Little Thatches) which may look private but is, in fact, a right of way. Follow the path around the edge of the garden to join a minor road where you bear left to follow it briefly uphill to the church.

St Mary's Church in Ashley dates to the 12th century and stands within the earthworks of Gains Castle, dating from Norman times but now long vanished. After admiring the church and old fort site, return to the point where you entered the woodland strip from the field and bear southeastwards (a right turn from this direction) as the path skirts the buildings of Ashley Glebe Farm, before exiting the woodland to continue past a small brick cottage. Here, you join a waymarked unplanted strip (a right of way) through a field.

About 400m ahead, at the eastern edge

of the field, you cross a farm track and continue straight on, passing old farm paraphernalia and a stand of oaks. The route then proceeds along a wide track at the edge of a field to skirt the northern margin of a small woodland.

Just beyond the woodland, the path continues next to some mature trees, at the end of which you can take the track branching right to the site of a Roman settlement. Returning to the mature trees, carry on along the track that leads gently downhill towards the old pumphouse that you passed earlier. Turn right when you emerge onto the bridleway just beyond the pumphouse to retrace your steps to the car park at Farley Mount.

◀ St Mary's Church at Ashley

Farley Mount Country Park

Distance 5km **Time** 1 hour 30
Terrain paths through woodland; some
hills, but none particularly demanding
Map OS Explorer OL32 **Access** no public
transport to the start; car park at the
start of the walk

Farley Mount Country Park is a large area
of deciduous woodland and downland
named after a folly commemorating the
landowner's prize-winning horse, a beast
pragmatically named 'Beware Chalk Pit',
which sped to victory in 1734.

Within the woodland is the site of
a Roman villa, which was excavated
between 1965 and 1972. The dig revealed a
near-complete geometric mosaic which is
now on display in Winchester Museum.
The villa was constructed in phases
between the 2nd and 5th centuries,
initially as a simple farmhouse. Later
additions, including a bathroom, indicate
that the inhabitants lived in relative
comfort. The building was seemingly
abandoned when the Romans left Britain.

There are several car parks giving access
to Farley Mount Country Park. This walk
starts from the car park next to some
prehistoric tumulus, due south of the site
of the Roman villa. At the western end of
the car park is an information panel and
vehicle barrier. Turn right, skirting the
barrier and ignoring the paths just
beyond on the right to carry on along the
wide stony track heading downhill.

Around 250m from the first vehicle
barrier, go around another barrier to
continue straight ahead. At a crossroads
of tracks about 250m after the second
vehicle barrier, continue straight ahead
once again. On this next section, you pass
through the site of the Roman villa, which
is maintained as an open glade within the
woodland. There are no above-ground
remains to be seen. Keep straight ahead at
the junction of several paths that shortly
follows the site.

Soon after, take the wide well-used path
leading off to the right to now start
heading east. In just over 200m, you come

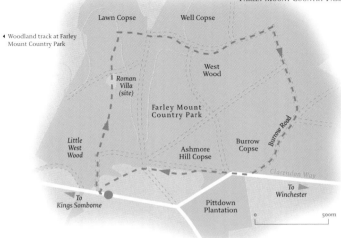

◀ Woodland track at **Farley Mount Country Park**

Lawn Copse

Well Copse

West Wood

Roman Villa (site)

Farley Mount Country Park

Little West Wood

Burrow Copse

Burrow Road

Ashmore Hill Copse

Clarendon Way

To Kings Somborne

Pittdown Plantation

To Winchester

0   500m

to a junction of several paths where you continue straight ahead onto a wide gravel vehicle track. Branch right at a junction just ahead, climbing slightly uphill. Stay on this wide track and avoid the more minor tracks leading off from it.

When you arrive at another junction, bear right to continue on the wide gravel vehicle track, which rises slightly and now takes you in a southeasterly direction before emerging at another junction of paths next to a Forestry Commission information panel in just over 550m.

Bear left at the information panel to go around a vehicle barrier and then take an immediate right to follow an ancient track (Burrow Road), characterised by earthen banks on each side. Branches overhang the track with adjacent wire fences on each side. Stay on this track as it bears southwest and avoid routes leading off it.

Some 500m after joining the track, you reach a road. Turn right here to enter a parking area at an entrance to Burrow Copse (not marked on OS maps). Bear left next to the vehicle barrier to continue on a footpath next to the road.

At a junction of paths in just over 100m, go through a gate to enter Pitt Down, a chalk grassland which is home to an array of specialist insect and plant species, including several rare species of butterfly. When you reach the bottom of the hill, pass through a couple of kissing gates linked by a grassy track, and continue straight on.

Very soon the route bears left on a wide grassy track which rises diagonally uphill. At the top of the slope, go through a kissing gate and turn left to return to the car park at the start of the walk.

41

Ampfield Woodland

Distance 6km **Time** 1 hour 30
Terrain mostly level and graded
woodland paths **Map** OS Explorer 131
Access no public transport to the start;
car park at the start of the walk on
Jermyns Lane

**Ampfield Woodland is a popular spot
about 3.5km northeast of Romsey. This
is a perfect leg-stretcher on level ground
within predominantly conifer woodland.
Orchids line the paths in summer and
the woodland is also a haven for
butterflies and day-flying moths.**

From the parking area on Jermyns Lane,
head past the vehicle barrier to enter the
woodland, as indicated by the waymarker.
Ignore the path leading off to the right
about 400m ahead and continue on the
wide forest track. About 600m from the
parking area the path swings almost 90°
to the right. Ignore any trails peeling off

from the most-used wide path, including
the broad track branching off to the right
about 600m after the 90° turn.

The path starts to head slightly uphill,
then levels off. Beware – the clay soil of
this bridleway may be slick after rain.
At a junction almost 2km from the car
park, take the middle of three paths and
keep going straight on, skirting some
wooden rails which prevent vehicle access.

As the path starts to rise gently again,
it enters a compartment of woodland
dominated by broadleaf tree species.
Keep going straight ahead and avoid
routes leading off from the main path.
About 900m after the wooden rails you
come to a T-junction, where you turn
right to follow the wide forest road
(Claypit Road on OS maps). A wooden
rail fence is to the left of the path.

Claypits were once a common feature in
western Hampshire. The first brickmakers

◀ Lichen-clad waymarker in Ampfield Woodland

in Hampshire were the Romans, who used the local clay to make roof tiles, bricks and hollow tiles for their hypocaust central heating systems – underfloor and sometimes interwall flue systems that heated the whole building from a single subterranean heat source, usually a boiling cauldron. After the Romans departed, the brick and tile industry ceased until the 14th century, when the Normans began firing clay for building purposes. The Romans weren't the first to create these systems, however. At Mohenjo-daro, one of the earliest and largest cities of the Indus River Valley in

what is now Pakistan, excavations have revealed underfloor heating systems built in around 2500BC, which is more than 2000 years before the beginning of the Roman Empire. Only in very recent years have we rediscovered the efficiency of underfloor heating systems here.

Ignore the grassy track bearing off to the right around 400m ahead and instead keep going. At a T-junction, turn right and drop gently downhill. Continue on this wide track for 2km and ignore all paths that lead off it. When you meet another T-junction, bear left to walk the 400m back to the car park.

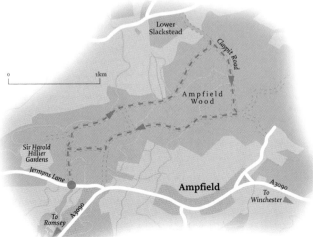

Houghton

**Distance 6.5km Time 2 hours
Terrain unsurfaced lanes and gentle
gradients; a section of farm track
Map OS Explorer 131 Access buses from
Stockbridge and Winchester; on-street
parking in the centre of Houghton and
just south of the village pub**

This walk provides pleasing views and in
summer the hedgerows are brimming
with insect life. The size of Houghton's
human population hasn't changed much
in the last 900 years and it is a designated
conservation area.

A parking bay about 70m south of the
village pub, the Boot Inn, marks the start
of this walk. From the parking bay, cross
the road to head up a narrow waymarked
footpath which leads between a hedge
and a fence. After a short distance, you
come to a waymarker where you go left
to follow the path behind some gardens.

This soon crosses a driveway where you
continue on the path straight ahead
before going across an unsurfaced track.
Carry on past a recreation ground and
turn right onto a street (Stevens Drove).
At the end of this, continue straight ahead
on the unsurfaced lane for 2km.

In summer months you should see a
variety of butterflies, damselflies, bees,
hoverflies and small birds. It's a relatively
long and straight stretch without views at
this point, but the hedgerows have high
biodiversity value and it is well worth
taking some moments in the warmer
months to walk slowly and enjoy the
presence of so many winged beasts. In
recent years insect and bird populations
have declined dramatically across England,

◄ An environmental stewardship field margin

so hedgerows such as these offer a sanctuary to these beleaguered creatures.

A bench at the T-junction at the end of the lane makes a good spot to enjoy the lane for 800m, then bear left at the waymarker indicating the Clarendon Way, which climbs a few steps. The views open out here and you can appreciate the rolling farmland that characterises the Hampshire countryside as the route continues unencumbered by hedges.

Carry straight on ahead when you meet a gravel track and take the time to admire the levels of plant biodiversity in the environmental stewardship field margins during the summer, when they are awash with colour.

After 2km you join an asphalt lane. Just before a wooden shed, turn left onto the field-side track. A hedge and trees are on your right with some houses beyond them. When you reach a field gate, bear right onto the track running between the field's fence and a hedge to meet a road (Stevens Drove). Cross this and continue straight on to retrace your steps to the start of the walk.

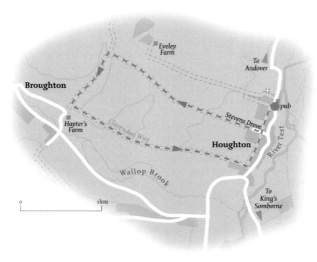

Northern Hampshire is often overlooked for the more obvious charms of the New Forest and the south, but it is certainly worth exploring. The range of walks in this region take you through shimmering fields, a billowing patchwork landscape sprinkled with ancient copses and woodlands, striated by hedges and dotted with grand old trees. It is a walkers' wonderland and home to an abundance of wildlife.

Tackling the ridge of Pilot Hill with the sweeping vista of Berkshire countryside unfolding as you gain height is just one of the must-do experiences in this area. The woodland at Greywell, with its twisted veteran oaks and beeches and sun-dappled glades flushed with ferns, is perhaps one of the most stunning in Hampshire, while at Ashford Hill you will find a land that time forgot, a remnant of a downland ecosystem that was common until the mid-20th century. All the walks

here are special, however, and represent the scenic diversity that the region has to offer.

The author Jane Austen was born in 1775 in Steventon, just a few miles from Basingstoke, and she drafted her most celebrated novel *Pride and Prejudice* while living in the area. She was known to have enjoyed going into Basingstoke for dances and shopping but spent her last few years on her brother's estate at Chawton, now a museum and well worth a visit. Austen died in Winchester in 1817 and is buried in the cathedral.

Burberry, the 160-year-old global fashion brand, was the brainchild of a Basingstoke man. Thomas Burberry was an apprentice draper from Basingstoke who, at the tender age of 21, established a process for waterproofing yarn and cloth after a chance conversation with a shepherd. The first Burberry store opened in Basingstoke on Winchester Street in 1856.

Racehorse training track near Kingsclere ▶

Hart and Basingstoke & Deane

Pamber Forest

Distance 3.5km **Time** 1 hour
Terrain mostly level forest tracks
Map OS Explorer 159 **Access** buses from
Basingstoke and Tadley stop at Pamber
Heath; car park at the start of the walk

**Pamber Forest is a 214-hectare ancient
woodland that dates back to at least
Norman times and is a remnant of the
once extensive Royal Forest of Windsor.
The forest is of exceptional wildlife
interest. Forty species of butterfly have
been recorded here, including white
admiral, silver-washed fritillary and
purple emperor.**

Pamber Forest has been a Site of Special
Scientific Interest since the 1950s and a
significant area of the reserve is managed
by selective thinning, whereby a
proportion of the trees are removed to
enable sufficient sunlight to reach the
forest floor. Rotational coppicing is also
practised, thereby enabling a diverse
range of plants to flourish. Coppicing was
a common feature of woodland
management in Europe for centuries and
provided a range of materials. It also
benefits plants and wildlife by creating a
range of habitat types. Some species of
plants are associated with ancient woods,
particularly coppiced woodlands that have
received years of active management.
Coppicing is often practised in ancient
woodlands nowadays to ensure that these
rare plant communities continue to
thrive. Keep your eyes peeled for red kites,
jays, woodpeckers and buzzards. If you are
lucky, you might see an adder.

From the car park at the southern end of
Impstone Road, a waymarker just beyond

◄ Southern hawker dragonfly

an information panel indicates a wide track leading into the woodland. The track's earthen banks suggest that this is a former droving route. Follow the track as it heads slightly downhill to reach a crossroads after about 550m.

Go straight across this to continue over a footbridge and, after about 700m, meet another crossroads near the corner of a fence. Here, you turn right and pass a nature reserve sign. Stay on the main track, avoiding any routes peeling off.

After crossing a cattle grid, continue straight ahead for 300m to a crossroads of paths, where you turn right onto a wide gravel track. Continue on this track for just over 800m, going straight through a crossroads of paths, before exiting the woodland into a grass recreation area.

Bear right on the thin gravel path that runs adjacent to the edge of the woodland and follows the course of some overhead powerlines. Continue following the path as it swings uphill to the left, away from the powerlines. Some allotments are visible on your right.

Join the access track for the allotments, still heading uphill. A few metres ahead

the track swings 90° to the left. Here you bear right, following a mown path near the back of some houses for about 100m. Bear slight left to join a path next to some garden fences, shortly turning left into an asphalt alley between houses. Turn right at the top of the alley onto a street (Burney Bit) and continue for a further 200m to return to the car park.

Impstone Road

Pamber Heath

Burney Bit

Lord's Wood

allotments

To Basingstoke

Heath Copse

Beggars Bridge Copse

String Lane Copse

Pamber Forest

Frame Green Copse

Gravelpit Copse

0   500m

49

Kingsclere

Distance 5km **Time** 1 hour 30
Terrain field-side paths and a horse
gallop; gently undulating with a couple
of steep sections **Map** OS Explorer 144
Access buses from Tadley, Basingstoke
and Newbury; car park in Kingsclere,
on-street parking is also available

The name Kingsclere is derived from
Old English and most likely refers to
a clearing in a royal hunting forest.
The Anglo-Saxon King Alfred mentioned
Kingsclere in his will in the 9th century.
Part of this walk passes along Freemantle
Park Down, which was part of the 13th-
century King John's lodge.

Exit Anchor Yard car park and bear left
to head up Anchor Road. As the road
swings to the right, continue straight
ahead on an alleyway between houses.

Turn left at the top of the alleyway onto
Pearces Place, then bear right to enter the
grassy recreation ground. Head diagonally
left towards some goalposts as you climb
uphill across the grounds.

Just beyond the goalposts a track exits
the recreation ground to the left via a gap
in the hedge. Follow this track for about
350m until you meet an unsurfaced lane,
where you turn right. At a junction about
500m ahead, keep going straight on,
ignoring the path to the right.

After a short distance, go straight ahead
through a gap in the hedge to follow a
waymarked path next to a wire fence.
Avoid the track that follows the hedge
round to the left. A horse gallop is visible
to the right as you proceed through an
area of open field for just under 1km,
heading towards the hill topped with a

◂ Looking north from Freemantle Park Down

row of Scots pine (Freemantle Park Down). The radio station on top of the hill sits on the site of Freemantle Park, formerly a royal lodge. King John is recorded as staying here for a couple of nights in August 1209.

Not long after the path starts to head uphill, go right through an easily missed kissing gate to follow the path, which ascends diagonally across the flank of the hill. The path levels off just below the row of Scots pine near the top of the hill, and you are rewarded with fine views of Kingsclere and the countryside that surrounds the village.

About 700m after the kissing gate, bear right on the track that begins to descend the hillside. After around 400m, the path levels out at the bottom of the hill. Here, you bear right to leave the woodland and continue along the horse gallop directly ahead. If it happens to be in use during your walk, you should avoid the gallop and walk on the grass next to it and if you are walking with a dog, keep it on a leash.

Follow the gallop for about 1km until you meet a lane, which you cross and continue straight ahead up some steps. After a few metres the path emerges into the recreation ground you crossed earlier. Continue straight ahead, passing the goalposts. At the bottom of the slope, you emerge onto Pearces Place and head back to Anchor Yard car park.

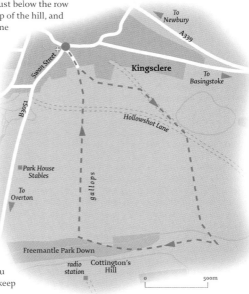

Ashford Hill

Distance 4.5km **Time** 1 hour 30
Terrain grassy tracks and woodland
paths; some short but steep slopes
Map OS Explorer 159 **Access** buses from
Basingstoke, Kingsclere, Tadley and
Headley; car park off Chapel Lane
in Ashford Hill

Ashford Hill is a National Nature Reserve
and, due to its relatively remote location
with limited car parking, it receives few
visitors. However, it's a real gem with a
varied complex of woodlands and
agriculturally unimproved meadows
lying in a broad shallow valley.

According to Natural England, the
reserve is without comparison in central
southern England for its habitat quality,
diversity of communities and number of
rare and threatened species. This is one
of the few remaining of these habitats
once widespread in lowland England, and

a walk here offers a window to a rural past.

From the car park at the entrance to the
recreation area, follow Chapel Lane to the
main road (B3051) and turn left to follow
the pavement downhill. Just before the
road crosses a stream, bear right onto a
footpath waymarked as the Brenda Parker
Way, opposite the signposted Old Lane, to
enter the nature reserve via a meadow
surrounded by woodland. The path fades
as you forge through long grass in warmer
months. Keep going directly ahead until
you come to a wooden footbridge on your
left about 450m after entering the reserve.

Cross this bridge and continue straight
ahead (now heading north) across the
field to a kissing gate where you turn
right. Here, the path becomes more
obvious, shortly diving into woodland
and starting to climb. The path leaves the
nature reserve here before re-entering it
further on.

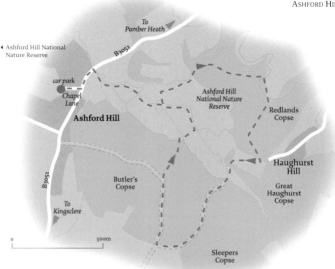

To
Pamber Heath

B3051

◀ Ashford Hill National
Nature Reserve

car park

Chapel
Lane

Ashford Hill

Ashford Hill
National Nature
Reserve

Redlands
Copse

Haughurst
Hill

B3051

Butler's
Copse

Great
Haughurst
Copse

To
Kingsclere

0   500m

Sleepers
Copse

When you come to a T-junction, turn right. The path soon starts to descend. Keep to the most obvious route, ignoring trails that branch off to the left. After crossing a stream, the path climbs up an embankment. When you reach the top, turn right to follow the footpath across a meadow.

After about 200m, cross a small bridge and continue straight on. Don't take the path to the right which leads back into the reserve, or any other routes that appear less used than the path you are already following.

At a junction of paths about 500m beyond the bridge, ignore the track to the left with a vehicle barrier across it and continue straight on. In a short while, you come to another junction of paths. Here, you bear right and duck under a metal vehicle barrier. There is no waymarker, but it is a right of way.

Stay on the footpath going straight ahead and avoid paths leading off it. About 400m after the vehicle barrier you come to a fork, where you bear right. After another 200m you re-enter the reserve and bear right to cross a small boardwalk, continuing across the meadow to reach a footbridge.

Don't cross this but bear left when facing the bridge. After about 250m you pass the footbridge you crossed earlier. This time ignore it and continue straight ahead to retrace your steps to the start of the walk.

53

Pilot Hill

Distance 5.5km **Time** 1 hour 45
Terrain mostly steep estate tracks
Maps OS Explorer 144, 131 **Access** no
public transport to the start; if you
intend to visit The Jack Russell Inn you
may park in the pub car park at the
landlord's discretion, otherwise there
is very limited roadside parking in the
village: please park considerately

**At 286m, Pilot Hill is the highest hill in
Hampshire and it lies within the North
Wessex Downs Area of Outstanding
Natural Beauty. While the walk is a
simple linear route from the pub or
village to the escarpment and back,
the views are sublime.**

The pub at the start of the walk – The
Jack Russell – is an elegant establishment
with a large garden overlooking a pond.
During the cooler months, a drink in front
of one of its woodburners is a great way
to round off this invigorating walk. The
beginning of the walk is in the Test Valley
district, but the summit lies within
Basingstoke and Deane.

From The Jack Russell, return to the
road that runs through the village and
turn left. Continue past the church and a
grand house, turning right as indicated by
the waymarker just after passing the
Faccombe Estate office. Continue on an
asphalt drive, which becomes an
unsurfaced lane and begins to descend
the hillside.

At the waymarker a short way ahead,
continue straight on, avoiding the tracks
leading off to the right and left. After

about 500m or so, continue straight ahead at the crossroads. (None of the other routes are public rights of way.)

Follow the track as it starts to climb steeply up the hill with wind turbines on your left. The first of these was erected in the 1980s, making the Faccombe Estate one of the first estates in Britain to install a wind turbine. Follow the track for just over 1km as it continues to ascend. The rolling countryside in this secluded notch of Hampshire makes for pleasant viewing.

On reaching a stile, go left into the field and over another stile straight ahead, through a small clump of trees and vegetation. Continue straight on along the unplanted strip through the field. A magnificent view unfolds as you approach the rim of the escarpment. If the field atop Pilot Hill is planted with crops, you won't be able to reach the trig point that marks the summit. After marvelling at the view, head back the way you came for refreshment at The Jack Russell.

◄ Heading towards the summit of Pilot Hill

Bramshill Plantation

Distance 6km **Time** 1 hour 30
Terrain mostly level graded forest roads
Map OS Explorer 159 **Access** no public
transport to the start; car park at the start
of the walk, 6km west of Yateley

The Freshwater Habitats Trust has
categorised Bramshill Plantation as a
'Flagship Pond Site' and it is a great
habitat for nightjar, Dartford warbler,
jays and woodlark. Be warned – there are
numerous tracks through the forest and
since it is almost entirely flat there are
very few points of reference. Pay careful
attention to your location.

Start from the car park, which is just
past the western boundary of St Neot's
prep school grounds on the opposite side
of Bramshill Road from some pylons.

From the car park, take the path leading
directly under the powerlines; the path
then bears left across the treeless strip
below the powerlines. A short distance
from the car park, turn left to follow
the track through woodland.

Carry on along this for 250m until it
joins an asphalt track, where you turn
right. After a further 200m you come to a
crossroads, where you continue straight
ahead. The track swings sharp right
further ahead before the asphalt ends and
you carry on along the wide graded forest
track, ignoring any narrower more minor
tracks further on.

After 600m you arrive at a pond. Despite
its silt-laden water, it is a haven for a
variety of winged creatures. Ignore the
first forestry track leading off to the right

but take the next one to the right 30m ahead. About 150m after you turn right, the track joins a wider track where you bear left.

Some 150m further on, you arrive at a path junction at a larger pond. Bear right here, skirting the edge of the water, to continue for another 350m to a crossroads of tracks.

Turn left at the crossroads and ignore the path peeling off to the left after 130m. A short distance ahead follow the track as it takes you 90° to the right, ignoring the path that veers off to the right further on.

At a T-junction, turn left and avoid going through the vehicle barrier onto the road. Follow this track, now heading westwards, before bearing left to go over a small footbridge with wooden rails, ignoring the track to the right just before the bridge.

After walking for another 150m (you're now heading south on the return route), you will spy a track leading off to the right. Follow this a short way as it provides access to another pond, larger than the previous two. Keep your eyes peeled for deer at the water's edge. You may also see coots or moorhens here.

After viewing the pond, return to the wider track for a long straight march, continuing straight ahead at a crossroads in an open treeless area.

In another 25om, the track swings to the right and then comes to a T-junction, where you bear left. A little further on, you go through a crossroads: carry straight on for 50om until you come to a T-junction. Turn left here to join a wide track, now heading east for 50om and ignoring tracks bearing left – the second of these is the asphalt track you took earlier. From this point, retrace your steps to the wide unplanted strip under the powerlines, bearing right to return to the car park at the start.

◀ Pond at Bramshill Plantation

Hartley Wintney

Distance 5km **Time** 1 hour 30
Terrain mostly level paths
Map OS Explorer 144 **Access** buses from
Reading, Hook, Alton, Camberley,
Aldershot and Fleet; limited on-street
parking after the golf club entrance on
Park Corner Road in Hartley Wintney

This walk tours Hazeley Heath, one of
the region's largest tracts of heathland.
As a Special Protected Area, it is home
to some rare birds such as nightjar,
woodlark and Dartford warbler, and
some rare plants such as the carnivorous
sundew. You may also spot fallow deer
here. Some of the paths described in
this route may not be waymarked

The walk starts from the beginning of
Hunts Common, a residential street
branching off and running parallel to the
A30 as it leaves Hartley Wintney heading

north. Walk along the row of houses
lining the street to find a waymarked
footpath next to Hunters Lodge, which
has a red postbox outside.

This path climbs slightly as it takes you
between houses and parking areas to
enter a gloomy woodland dominated by
laurel, lime, yew, holly and oak. Stay on
the widest path, passing some old
earthworks as the terrain levels out.

Now on a wide gravel path, continue
straight ahead to meet an unsurfaced
vehicle track in just over 700m. Here, an
RSPB information panel provides details
of some of the wildlife that can be found
at Hazeley Heath. Cross the track and
continue straight ahead for about 200m to
meet an asphalt road.

Turn briefly right onto the road and
then left to continue on a path. Keep an
eye out for the aspen, one of Britain's

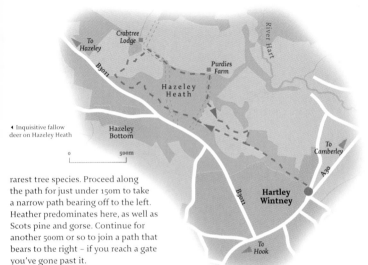

◄ Inquisitive fallow
deer on Hazeley Heath

rarest tree species. Proceed along
the path for just under 150m to take
a narrow path bearing off to the left.
Heather predominates here, as well as
Scots pine and gorse. Continue for
another 500m or so to join a path that
bears to the right – if you reach a gate
you've gone past it.

After about 200m, you come to a
waymarker where you bear right, before
going left at the bridleway waymarker a
short distance ahead. In just over 150m,
the bridleway reaches an unsurfaced lane
at the entrance to a large house (Crabtree
Lodge). Bear right onto the lane.

About 270m ahead, the lane passes
the entrance for Wedgewood Farm before
reaching the entrance to Purdies Farm,
where you turn right onto the gravel
track waymarked with a yellow arrow.
After walking another 250m, bear left to
pass two concrete bollards and, at the
junction just beyond, continue straight
on. Ignore the path branching off to the
left and head straight through the two
sets of crossroads.

At the next path junction, continue
straight on, ignoring the path to the
right. A little further on, an old military
structure and a steep concrete slope just
beyond mark the spot where winch
practice was undertaken during the
Second World War. Bear right on the
concrete track and pass a couple of
discarded tank caterpillar tracks.

Around 150m after the caterpillar tracks
you meet the wide track that you walked
along earlier. Bear left here and retrace
your steps to the start. Make sure you
continue straight ahead just past the old
earthworks rather than taking the path
to the right.

Greywell

Distance 5.5km **Time** 1 hour 30
Terrain mostly flat paths through
woodland and parkland
Map OS Explorer 144 **Access** buses from
Basingstoke and Long Sutton; on-street
parking at Greywell

Greywell epitomises rural Hampshire
and has proudly held the titles of Best
Kept Village in Hampshire and Best Small
Village in Hampshire. This walk starts
and ends at the Fox and Goose, the
quaint village pub, and wanders through
an ancient semi-natural woodland just
north of the village.

When facing the Fox and Goose, bear
left to follow the main village street past
some charming Tudor-era cottages
(there's an impressive number of listed
buildings in Greywell). A little way south
of the pub, turn right onto a narrow
footpath next to an ivy-clad house called
The Malthouse to enter a small field.

The path takes you straight ahead

through the field to a stile. After crossing
this bear right to follow the path around
the field edge.

At the top of the field, go through a gap
in the fence and turn left into a parkland
landscape studded with mature oaks.
Follow the waymarker to head slightly
uphill, heading diagonally left across the
parkland on a faint route for about 200m,
aiming for a fingerpost next to an
impressive oak.

Bear left at the waymarker and head
towards a huge felled tree trunk which
has been left here for wildlife habitat
purposes. Just beyond the trunk is a gate
next to a large standing oak. Go through
the gate to enter woodland, dropping
slightly downhill.

Cross two forest roads within a few
metres of each other and continue
straight ahead. The earthworks on your
right indicate the location of the
Basingstoke Canal tunnel. The canal was
opened in 1794 and closed to commercial

Evening light
at Greywell

vessels in 1910 after years of
financial loss. The tunnel is home to
the largest winter bat roost in England.

At the path junction about 100m after
passing the forest roads, continue straight
ahead, following the blue arrow
waymarker. Just over 500m beyond the
path junction you meet a road, which
continues straight ahead before sweeping
round to the right, heading downhill.

When the asphalt ends, continue
straight ahead on an unsurfaced lane,
crossing the former canal via a bridge.
About 600m beyond the bridge, bear right
to go over a stile just before an overpass
of the M3 motorway and continue
straight ahead adjacent to a wooden
fence. The path may be a bit overgrown
at this point.

Further on, the path swings right and
joins a forest track. Continue straight
ahead on this track, then bear left at a
fingerpost after a short distance to pass
an old wooden hut surrounded by grand
oaks, beech and holly.

About 650m beyond the hut, bear right
where converging tracks form a triangle
of woodland, then follow the track as it
swings to the right just ahead, as
indicated by a waymarker. Continue
straight ahead for about 400m and bear
left when the route joins a track merging
from the right. Keep going straight on, as
indicated by another waymarker.

Cross a stile next to a pair of gates
about 300m after passing the waymarker
and continue straight ahead through the
gate 250m ahead. When you meet a
waymarked crossroads of paths, go left.
Here you leave the woodland and return
to the parkland you crossed earlier. Bear
diagonally left across the parkland and
retrace your steps to the start of the walk,
keeping an eye out for the easily missed
stile near The Malthouse.

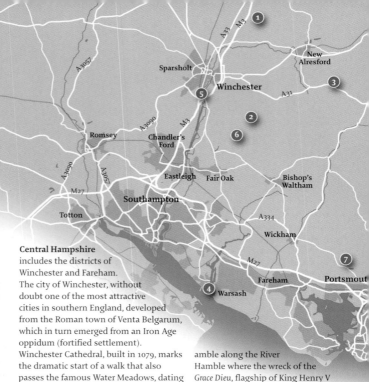

Central Hampshire
includes the districts of
Winchester and Fareham.
The city of Winchester, without
doubt one of the most attractive
cities in southern England, developed
from the Roman town of Venta Belgarum,
which in turn emerged from an Iron Age
oppidum (fortified settlement).
Winchester Cathedral, built in 1079, marks
the dramatic start of a walk that also
passes the famous Water Meadows, dating
back to medieval times.

Hampshire's quintessential rolling
farmland features in several of these
walks, with the impressively named
natural amphitheatre of Cheesefoot Head
forming the start point of one such route.
There are some enchanting woodland
wanders which are a delight at any time of
year and provide important habitat and
food for a variety of bird species, while for
invigorating sea air you can't beat an

amble along the River
Hamble where the wreck of the
Grace Dieu, flagship of King Henry V
of England, lies beneath the surface.
Launched in 1418, this was one of the
largest ships in the world at the time. It
seems the hapless vessel only sailed one
voyage, during which the crew mutinied
both before leaving port and while at sea,
forcing the ship to dock permanently at
the Isle of Wight. The ship was eventually
towed to a mooring in the River Hamble
where she was struck by lightning and set
ablaze in 1439.

Winchester and Fareham

Micheldever Wood

Distance 3km **Time** 1 hour
Terrain almost level paths and graded
forest roads **Map** OS Explorer OL32
Access no public transport to the start;
car park at the start of the walk

The 217-hectare Micheldever Wood
contains a unique collection of
archaeological features dating from the
prehistoric to the medieval period. Due
to continuous woodland coverage and a
lack of ploughing since medieval times,
many of these features remain in a
fantastic state of preservation.

This route follows an archaeological
trail within the woodland and visits some
of these historic sites. The woods are
stunning in spring, with a profusion of
bluebells carpeting the forest floor. The
effect is even more spectacular against the
backdrop of towering mature beech near
the car park. This walk starts at two
information panels at the edge of the car
park. From the car park, bear left onto a
wide forest track. (Before you set out it's
worth taking a detour along the path
directly behind the panels into a
magnificent Tolkienesque beech
woodland. Return to the panels and take
the forest track as described above.) After
about 100m swing right to begin heading
north. In another 500m, just before the
track swings to the right again, leave the
track to continue straight ahead on a
narrower path.

A short way ahead, the convolutions in
the ground indicate an Iron Age
enclosure. At a T-junction beyond the
enclosure, go left, then turn right after a
brief distance to take a broad track

◄ Majestic beech trees at Micheldever Wood

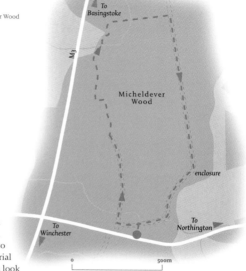

dropping downhill. After a short walk you arrive at an interpretation panel next to a tree-covered Iron Age burial mound. Once you've had a look around the mound, continue on the path.

Around 150m further on, some old earthen field boundaries are visible just to the left of the path, and some 100m beyond these you meet a junction of three paths where you bear right.

On meeting a wide graded forest road after around 350m, turn right to begin the long straight march southwards towards the start, ignoring minor routes leading off either side of the road. This eventually brings you to an information panel adjacent to a 'banjo enclosure', dating to the Iron Age – its name is derived from the banjo-like shape which consists of a

small round area with a long entrance track leading inward from one direction. The original purpose of banjo enclosures remains unclear. Surprisingly, the forest road goes right through the middle of the enclosure, a legacy of times when historical sites were treated with much less regard than nowadays.

After looking around the enclosure, which may be somewhat obscured by long grass in warmer months, continue straight ahead past the information panel to eventually meet the car park at the start of the walk.

Cheesefoot Head

Distance 6.5km **Time** 1 hour 30
Terrain unsurfaced lanes, concrete tracks
and field-edge paths; moderately steep
hillsides **Map** OS Explorer OL32
Access the South Downs Rambler Bus
stops here in summer; car park on the
northern side of the A272, about 5km
east of Winchester

The quirkily named Cheesefoot Head,
also known as Matterley Bowl, was
shaped by meltwater eroding the soft
chalk strata at the end of the last ice age.
During the preparations for the D-Day
invasion of Normandy in the Second
World War, this natural amphitheatre
became a gathering point for US troops
who were stationed nearby.

Shortly before the Normandy landings
of 6 June 1944, General Eisenhower
addressed more than 100,000 troops here.
More recently this has been the site of
festivals such as The Glade, Sanctuary,
Boomtown and Homelands. This walk
starts and finishes near the amphitheatre,
but tours former downland to the south.
In summer you are likely to see streaks of
red poppies in the fields and hear the trill
of skylarks overhead.

From the car park, take the path that
parallels the A272. At the end of the path,
turn right and walk a short way for a view
of the natural amphitheatre of Cheesefoot
Head, before retracing your steps to a
crossing point of the A272, waymarked as
the South Downs Way. Cross the road

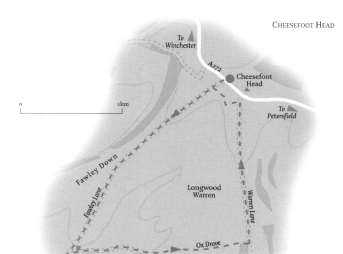

with caution and head downhill on the footpath directly opposite.

After about 150m or so, you arrive at a waymarked crossroads of paths. Continue straight ahead along the public bridleway. In about 1.5km, continue on the unsurfaced lane which is waymarked as a restricted byway.

The lane meets an asphalt track next to a cottage in just under 1km and here you head uphill on an unsurfaced lane to your left, waymarked as a bridleway. This former drove road, appropriately named Ox Drove, is flanked by hedges, hazel and gnarled ivy-clad oaks.

Where the path emerges from a small woodland onto a concrete track, bear right. After a few metres the track swings to the left and climbs uphill. The field edges have been left as environmental

margins, which benefit a number of plant and insect species. Corncrakes, which are a nationally rare bird with populations declining due to farming practices in recent years, have been spotted here.

After 1.5km of uphill walking on this concrete track, bear left onto another track just before a gate leading to the A272. This track drops downhill and then runs parallel to the A272. After 250m, bear right at a wooden sign indicating a footpath at the top of an open grassy area. Follow this path for about 150m to the crossroads of paths you encountered near the start of the walk.

Here you bear right to rejoin the South Downs Way and head uphill to the A272, which you cross to return to the car park.

◀ Wildflowers at Cheesefoot Head

Bramdean

Distance 8.5km **Time** 2 hours
Terrain unsurfaced lanes, forest roads,
woodland tracks and field-edge paths;
undulating but not particularly steep
Map OS Explorer OL32 **Access** the South
Downs Rambler Bus stops here in the
summer; no parking in Bramdean

This intriguing loop passes through
Cheriton Wood, site of the Battle of
Cheriton in 1644, in which Sir William
Waller's Roundheads were victorious.
Along the way you can also visit
Bramdean Church, a rare surviving
'tabernacle' – a church built from
corrugated iron on a timber frame – that
was assembled in just five days in 1883.

As there is no on-street parking, this
walk starts at the bus stops (there's one
on each side of the road) outside the Fox
Inn. Head west along the pavement beside
the A272. After a short walk, the pavement
becomes a gravel track. Cross the road

with caution just after a sign requesting
drivers to reduce their speed. Walk up the
unsurfaced Alresford Lane next to
Highways Cottage, ignoring the track
leading off to the right a few metres on.

After 1km, turn right onto a narrow
unwaymarked path between clumps of
hazel at the western edge of Cheriton
Wood. Keep your eyes peeled as this path
is easily missed: the entrance is opposite
a large beech tree. If you see a path
leading off to your left, you've overshot
and will need to retrace your steps.

It was here and just to the west of the
wood that the Battle of Cheriton Wood
took place on 29 March 1644. Although
regarded as an important victory for the
Parliamentarian army, in truth it was a
chaotic encounter with poor leadership
on both sides.

The path soon joins a wide track that
marches through the woods: continue
straight ahead on this for 1.5km and

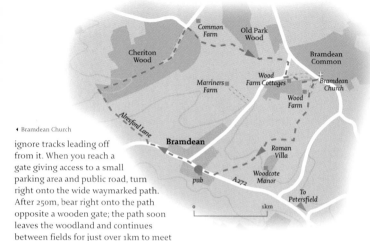

◀ Bramdean Church

ignore tracks leading off from it. When you reach a gate giving access to a small parking area and public road, turn right onto the wide waymarked path. After 250m, bear right onto the path opposite a wooden gate; the path soon leaves the woodland and continues between fields for just over 1km to meet a road, where you bear right.

Follow the roadside verge for 200m to Elm Cottage where a sign indicates a smokery. Follow the gravel track to the left, passing several houses (Wood Farm Cottages) with large gardens. At the end cottage, bear slightly left onto the grassy track opposite. Follow the track as it swings round to the right. After about 300m you arrive at a small parking area.

If you want to visit Bramdean Church, cross the road to the sign indicating the church and follow the path for about 150m. In Victorian times hundreds of these sheet-iron-clad churches were erected in remote places in Britain, with the intention that no-one would be without access to a church or priest. Other corrugated-iron buildings were available at the time, purchased via catalogues,

which included village halls and even railway stations.

From the church, return to the parking area and continue on the unsurfaced track, which joins the access road to Wood Farm. Just before the farmhouse, bear left to pass agricultural buildings and take a stony track which becomes a lane flanked by high hedges. Around 650m after the farm, bear right at an old barn to follow the path along the field edge.

About 400m after the old barn, cross a stile on your left and bear right to follow the yellow waymarker arrow into a small woodland. Just after leaving the woodland you'll see an old watertower belonging to Woodcote Manor.

When you meet the public road about 800m beyond the tower, bear right to return to the start of the walk.

Warsash

Distance 6.5km **Time** 1 hour 30
Terrain mostly level paths along the
River Hamble, and woodland paths
Map OS Explorer OL3 **Access** buses from
Southampton, Fareham, Gosport,
Stubbington, Itchen and Portchester;
car park available at the start of the walk

This walk takes you through Hook-with-
Warsash Local Nature Reserve which runs
alongside the River Hamble – a river that
was of great strategic importance during
the Hundred Years War with France in the
14th century. The route also tours the
landscaped Holly Hill Woodland Park,
which dates to around 1838.

The car park at the beginning of this
walk is located at the western end of
Passage Lane, next to Stone Pier Boatyard.
The walk starts next to the car park's

public toilets, where you join a riverside
path and head upriver with views across
to Hamble-le-Rice on the other side. The
river bristles with yacht masts and at low
tide the air is filled with the scent of
seaweed and tidal mudflats. The land to
the right of the path, which floods at high
tide, is known as Bunny Meadows. The
name has nothing to do with rabbits; it
refers to culverts known as 'bunnies'.

Continue on the riverside path for
2.5km, passing a couple of old wrecks
before reaching a gravel area surrounded
by wooden fences. Here, you turn right to
follow a waymarked path into woodland.
Carry on along this path, which joins an
asphalt lane (Crableck Lane), for a
distance of about 800m.

Turn right at the top of the lane onto a
suburban street (Holly Hill Lane). When

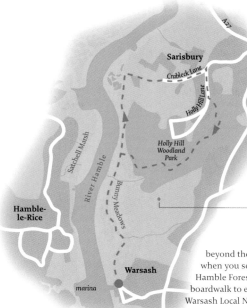

Sarisbury

Crableck Lane

Holly Hill Lane

Holly Hill Woodland Park

Satchell Marsh

River Hamble

Bunny Meadows

Hamble-le-Rice

0   1km

Warsash

marina

you are parallel with house number 84, look for the gate opposite which takes you onto a path leading away to the left. After following this path into Holly Hill Woodland Park, continue straight ahead downhill, skirting round two vehicle barriers and further on crossing a footbridge over a stream in an attractive grassy glade containing duckponds and bridges. Turn right immediately after the bridge to follow the edge of a pond. At a bench after about 200m, bear left.

Keep to this route for just over 500m, ignoring the bridge to the right a little beyond the bench. Turn right when you see a sign for the Hamble Foreshore and follow the boardwalk to enter Hook-with-Warsash Local Nature Reserve. Stay on the most obvious route here, passing magnificent old trees that were once part of an open parkland landscape belonging to Holly Hill mansion, which was demolished in the 1920s.

The path eventually exits the woodland and crosses an open area towards the River Hamble. Turn left at a T-junction of paths a short distance after passing a memorial bench. Follow this path back to the riverside path.

Turn left at the riverside to head back to the car park at the beginning of the walk. There's a pub, The Rising Sun, at 74 Shore Road, just south of the car park, if you're in need of refreshment.

◀ Old wreck on the River Hamble

Winchester

Distance 6.5km **Time** 1 hour 30
Terrain level walk along pavements and
riverside paths **Map** OS Explorer OL32
Access buses from Micheldever, Andover,
and Alton; car parks in Winchester

Winchester, Hampshire's striking county
town and the former capital city of
England, is steeped in history and
dominated by the sky-scraping steeples
of its medieval cathedral. The English
Romantic poet John Keats was inspired
by the beauty of the city when he wrote
his ode 'To Autumn' after staying here in
1819. This walk starts at the cathedral and
visits the stunning Water Meadows,
through which crystal-clear water has
been sluiced for more than 1000 years.

When facing the main cathedral doors,
bear right and head past a waymarker on
a lamppost indicating the cathedral's
historic Inner Close. Follow the path as it
continues alongside and around a lawn
to reach a parking area on Dome Alley
with a large Victorian building in
front of you. Here you bear
left and follow the

road as it swings right to pass through
the Priory Gate. Just beyond this, bear left
to pass through King's Gate. This was one
of the main entrances to the medieval
city. The Church of St Swithun-upon-
Kingsgate, which dates to at least the 13th
century, sits atop King's Gate and once
formed part of the city wall.

Turn left onto College Street and
continue past the modest townhouse
where author Jane Austen spent the last
few days of her life, then on past the grand
entrance to Winchester College and the
entrance to Wolvesey Castle. These
extensive ruins date largely from the

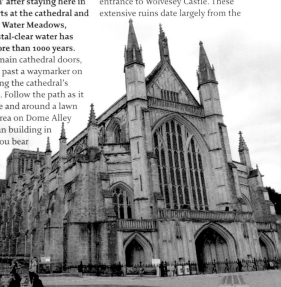

Winchester

12th-century palace of Bishop Henry of Blois, which was once one of the most eminent buildings in England. After passing the Pilgrims' School just ahead, the route continues on a cycle/pedestrian path, sweeping left before you bear right to follow the route signposted for St Catherine's Hill viewpoint and cross the River Itchen via a footbridge. Follow the road (Wharf Hill) round to the right and continue straight ahead, ignoring College Walk a few metres beyond Granville Place on the right, to join Domum Road.

Go right through a gate next to house no 3 to follow a path to a footbridge across the River Itchen, continuing downriver on the other side. In 250m go through a gate and carry straight on, following a waymarker for the Itchen Way.

At the roadbridge after 500m, go left to cross this and carry on along the path heading downriver. If you go under an old railway bridge, you've walked too far.

Shortly after joining a cyclepath, you'll see a gate and path on your left leading to St Catherine's Hill Nature Reserve. The hilltop chapel was built in the 13th century and the summit is worth a detour for the views of Winchester.

Some 600m after St Catherine's Hill, go right at a junction of tracks to follow the cycletrack signposted for St Cross, Stanmore and Twyford. Soon after passing a vehicle barrier on your left, take the footpath towards the waymarked Hospital of St Cross, a monastery with a

brotherhood of around 25 monks who also run a gift shop and tearoom (ahead left).

Continue straight ahead at a post with four waymarking discs to skirt the edge of the monastery, ignoring the path to the left (Clarendon Way) at a corner of the grounds. Views of the Water Meadows will be occasionally visible on your right.

Ignore the footbridge to a residential street and carry straight on to reach a road. Cross this and take the path opposite to its end in the grounds of Winchester College. Turn right, then left along an old brick wall. After about 100m, arrive at the entrance to Wolvesey Castle where you retrace your steps to the start.

◀ Winchester Cathedral

Owslebury

Distance 9.5km **Time** 2 hours 30
Terrain unsurfaced lanes, field paths and
along woodland strips; a few steep
sections but mostly gently undulating
Map OS Explorer OL32 **Access** buses from
Winchester; limited on-street parking is
available near the church; if you intend to
visit the Ship Inn, you may park in the
pub car park at the landlord's discretion

Owslebury's main street follows the line
of a Roman road which once travelled
from Winchester to the south coast near
Portchester. Part of this walk traces the
Roman road and starts at St Andrew's
Church, the last church in Hampshire to
hold Mass in Latin. This was brought to
an abrupt end when the priest was shot
dead at the altar during the English
Reformation in the 16th century.

Enter St Andrew's churchyard from the
main village road and follow the path
waymarked as the Pilgrim's Trail, which
leads to the unsurfaced Pitcot Lane. Turn
right to head downhill on this sometimes
slippery lane.

Where the lane ends, enter a field and
turn left to follow the waymarked
Pilgrim's Trail. The path swings to the
right after 200m, followed by a straight
stretch that traces the route of one of
several Roman roads that radiate out
from Winchester.

After crossing a minor road, continue
straight ahead, following the waymarked
track towards Phillips Farm. At the
farmyard gate the path turns right into a
field and enters a small woodland after
just a few metres. At a junction of paths,
continue straight ahead. This is part of

the Monarch's Way, a long-distance footpath, as well as the Pilgrim's Trail.

In just over 500m, the path exits the woodland onto a gravel track (Greenhill Lane). Here, you turn sharp left and continue for 1.5km to a minor public road, ignoring a track leading off to the right before you reach the road.

Turn briefly right onto the public road before crossing the road to go over a stile into a field opposite Greenhill Cottage. Head directly downhill from the stile to traverse three fields, each of which is accessed via a stile.

On meeting an asphalt lane, turn left to continue on the waymarked Allan King's Way. After about 600m you pass some cottages belonging to Lower Whiteflood Farm, where you keep going straight on for a further 500m to meet a minor road. Cross this and carry on along the waymarked bridleway opposite.

After 400m, at the top of what is now a narrow track, you enter a field. Continue on the path straight ahead and ignore the one leading off to the right. On the other side of the field you meet a public road. Cross this and continue on the track in front of you for 700m to emerge at a waymarked crossroads.

Bear left at the waymarker to follow the track (Honeyman Lane on OS maps) for 1km where you meet another minor road.

Cross this and continue straight ahead on the waymarked bridleway (Stags Lane).

After 750m the bridleway comes to a minor road opposite some cottages. Here, you bear left onto the roadside verge and continue for just over 500m until you see a kissing gate and waymarked footpath on your right. Follow the track for about 200m until you reach a residential street in Owslebury.

Turn right onto the street a few metres after going through a gate and follow the road as it swings round to the left. At the next junction of streets, turn right to return to the start of the walk.

◀ St Andrew's Church at Owslebury

Southwick

Distance 5km **Time** 1 hour 30
Terrain mostly level paths through
fields, and unsurfaced tracks
Map OS Explorer OL3 **Access** buses from
Cosham and Wickham; on-street parking
available and a public car park next to the
Golden Lion pub car park

This pleasant perambulation includes
paths through fields just to the north of
the village, with the option to visit the
remains of an Augustinian priory behind
the Golden Lion. All but one of
Southwick's houses are owned by the
Southwick Estate, as indicated by the
maroon colour of their front doors.

This walk starts and ends at the
Golden Lion pub, where the US General
Eisenhower (who later became US
President) and the British General
Montgomery would drink together during

the D-Day invasion preparations in the
Second World War.

When facing the pub, bear left to head
up the High Street. Continue straight
on through a set of crossroads, taking a
moment to admire the medieval Saint
Michael and All Angels Church, which
retains some elements of an earlier
Anglo-Saxon church. On coming to a
T-junction just after the Red Lion pub,
bear left onto Back Lane.

In 100m, turn right onto a gravel
driveway between hedges, waymarked as
a footpath next to Berry Meadow
Cottages. Just beyond a back garden join
a grassy path and continue for about
250m on an unplanted strip through two
fields to reach a minor public road.

Cross the road and continue through
the field in front of you. The path may be
faint and overgrown here. Head straight

◄ The ruins of Southwick Priory

across the field to a small footbridge and enter woodland just beyond the bridge. The entrance to the woodland path may be obscured by bracken, depending on the time of year. Continue straight ahead when you join a wide vehicle track.

After 350m, bear right to go through a kissing gate into a field (Walton Heath) and continue straight ahead for 500m across the field. You may need to unclip two electric fences before reattaching them behind you as you cross the field. These rubber-handled removable fence sections are designed to provide access through electric fences.

Once you've exited the field bear right to follow the public road as far as the driveway to Mitchelland Farm, where you bear left to follow the driveway before turning right onto a bridleway at the top of the access track to a couple of cottages.

Follow this bridleway for 700m to a minor road which connects Southwick with Denmead. Turn right and continue on the roadside verge for about 560m to reach the High Street, where you turn left and head back to the Golden Lion.

If you fancy seeing the remains of the priory, which was founded in the mid-12th century by King Henry I of England, follow the access road to the Golden Lion's car park. Cross the road just beyond the car park to enter the woodland opposite and follow the path for 350m. The building was destroyed during the Dissolution of the Monasteries in 1538 and only a short section of wall remains standing. The ruins are fenced and can be accessed via a gate. You can then follow the woodland path branching off to the left to complete a circuit of the woodland (unduly named 'The Wilderness') before heading back to the start of the walk.

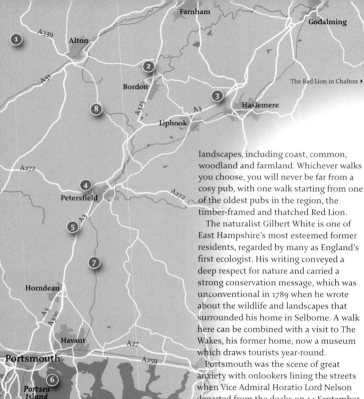

The Red Lion in Chalton ▸

landscapes, including coast, common, woodland and farmland. Whichever walks you choose, you will never be far from a cosy pub, with one walk starting from one of the oldest pubs in the region, the timber-framed and thatched Red Lion.

The naturalist Gilbert White is one of East Hampshire's most esteemed former residents, regarded by many as England's first ecologist. His writing conveyed a deep respect for nature and carried a strong conservation message, which was unconventional in 1789 when he wrote about the wildlife and landscapes that surrounded his home in Selborne. A walk here can be combined with a visit to The Wakes, his former home, now a museum which draws tourists year-round.

Portsmouth was the scene of great anxiety with onlookers lining the streets when Vice Admiral Horatio Lord Nelson departed from the docks on 14 September 1805 only to be killed at the Battle of Trafalgar weeks later. Earlier, in the 17th century, Portsmouth was the departure point of many who left Britain to settle on the east coast of North America, and the state of New Hampshire was formed in memory of the land they'd left behind. Today, Portsmouth remains an important naval base and commercial dock.

East Hampshire and Havant are the playground of Portsmouth's inhabitants and boast a delightful variety of walks. The routes in this chapter have been carefully chosen to include a range of

East Hampshire and Havant

Bentworth

Distance 8km **Time** 2 hours 30
Terrain paths through fields and
woodlands, and unsurfaced lanes; mostly
level, easy walking **Map** OS Explorer 144
Access buses from Basingstoke, Alton,
Lasham and Medstead; on-street parking
is available in front of the church on
Church Street

St Mary's Church at Bentworth is notable
for its unusual wooden belltower and the
royal coat of arms hanging inside the
church opposite the entrance. Royal
coats of arms were introduced to
churches by King Henry VIII when he
appointed himself head of the Church of
England in 1536. Also worthy of note is
the 13th-century font with a wooden dust
cover, dated 1605, and initials and dates
etched into the stonework of the porch.
The earliest inscribed is 1597.

From the parking area in front of the
church, walk back up the road and bear
left onto Church Street to pass some
quaint cottages and reach an open area
with picnic benches. Go right here onto
the waymarked footpath which leads off
from the right-hand corner of the picnic
area, beyond which is a fork where you
bear right to go through a gate and head
across a field to a kissing gate. From here,
follow the track through the adjacent field
to a minor road.

Cross the road and continue straight
ahead through the field, keeping the
hedge on your left. At the bottom corner
of the field, continue straight ahead on
the narrow path between a hedge and a
wire fence. The path soon turns a corner
and joins a grassy track between fields for
around 200m.

Turn right when you come to a path

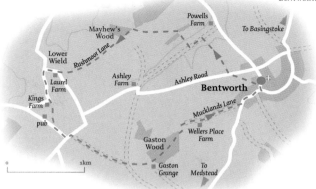

junction at the end of the field and head uphill on the vehicle track between fields to arrive at a waymarker after 250m. From here, bear left to cross the field diagonally via an unplanted strip. At an unsurfaced lane, turn right and then left at the junction a few metres ahead to follow the unsurfaced lane (Rushmoor Lane) for just over 1km to reach a minor public road.

Continue straight ahead on the road until, in around 200m, you emerge at a T-junction. Turn left here to head towards the signposted Upper Wield and Candover. Continue for 400m until the road curves 90° to the right, leaving the road at the bend to continue straight ahead on the footpath bordered by a leylandii hedge and wire fence.

Enter a field and follow the faint path which crosses to the bottom right-hand corner; you then angle left across the next field to a kissing gate, beyond which is a minor road.

If you fancy a drink or lunch, turn right to walk just a few metres to The Yew Tree

pub. Otherwise, bear left onto the road and at the junction ahead go left towards the signposted Bentworth and Bradley. After a few metres turn right onto a restricted byway with a vehicle barrier across its entrance. The raised embankments on each side indicate this lane is of some antiquity.

In around 800m you continue straight ahead through a couple of junctions of byways – one shortly after the other – to enter a field via a waymarked path leading through a gap in a hedge. Climb uphill through the field next to a deer fence. At the end of the fence, go through a gate to enter woodland, where you carry straight on along the waymarked route.

Bear left at the junction of paths in the woodland and keep following this path as it leaves the trees and joins an unsurfaced lane (Mucklands Lane). Continue on the lane until you meet a public road at Bentworth, where you bear left to return to St Mary's Church.

Kingsley

Distance 2.5km **Time** 30 minutes
Terrain mostly level woodland paths
and gently undulating sandy public
byways over Kingsley Common
Map OS Explorer 144 **Access** buses from
Basingstoke, Alton, Whitehill and
Haslemere; car park available at the
start of the walk

Kingsley Common must be one of
the most unique and visually impressive
commons in England. Some of the paths
are formed of golden sand, yet the plant
species that comprise this dry heath
habitat dazzle with myriad hues in
summer, while the gnarled veteran
oaks look oddly out of place against
this outlandish scene.

The car park is on the south side of
the main village street, opposite the
Kingsley Centre. Starting from the
information panel in the car park, head
towards Kingsley Pond, where you bear
right to follow the path around the pond.
In summer you may see ducks,
damselflies, moorhens, geese and lilies.

After passing a large house, bear left
onto an unsurfaced lane. After a few
metres the lane swings to the right and
passes several large houses. When you
encounter a Ministry of Defence sign,
follow the path to the right and then bear
left at the T-junction a short distance
ahead. In just 25m, continue on a lane to
your right, waymarked as a footpath. Once
past the entrance to Meadowgate Farm,
continue straight ahead on the grassy
track with fields on each side.

On reaching a junction in front of a
wooden fence after around 400m, turn
left. The path follows the field edge and
crosses a stream via a concrete bridge.
From here you continue on grassy
paths through a landscape of young

◄ Pond at Kingsley

broadleaves and open areas of grass.

About 100m after crossing the footbridge, continue straight ahead on the wide grassy track and ignore the path shortly leading off to the right. After a further 380m the track meets an unsurfaced road, where you bear left to cross a concrete bridge and continue to a path junction just inside the woodland ahead. Bear right onto the waymarked path here and stick to it, avoiding any of the more minor routes that may tempt you along the way. Around 300m beyond this path junction, you arrive at an open sandy area – a great spot for a picnic.

Bear left onto a sandy path, then after 50m go right. Continue over the crest of a hill, after which the path descends towards

some houses. As you near the foot of the hill you'll see a couple of paths leading off to the left. Take the one that leads directly under the powerlines. Where this path forks ahead bear right, then left to continue under the powerlines. Keeping to the widest path, ignore any minor paths leading off it until you arrive back at the car park

While you are in Kingsley, it is worth visiting the Kingsley Centre which supports disabled adults and provides opportunities for independence. A visit to the café and shop to see their good work is recommended.

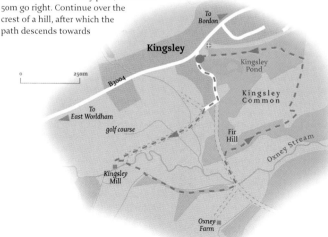

Waggoners Wells and Ludshott Common

**Distance 6km Time 2 hours
Terrain woodland trails, some quite
steep, and undulating stony paths over
commonland Map OS Explorer OL33
Access no public transport to the start;
car park at Waggoners Wells**

Waggoners Wells and Ludshott Common
are both reserves run by the National
Trust. Waggoners Wells is a series of
man-made ponds connected by a stream
set in a deep wooded valley. Ludshott
Common is the surviving half of the
ancient Manor of Ludshott, which dates
to Saxon times and is an SSSI known for
its variety of rare birds and other wildlife.

Head down the steps from the southern
end of the car park at the end of
Waggoners Wells Lane, then bear left onto
the path at the bottom of the steps. The
path passes through attractive broadleaf
woodland next to a sequence of three
ponds. It's worth pausing here for a while
to enjoy the ambience of this stunning
wooded valley. The ponds were created in
the 17th century to serve the local iron
industry but were never used as such.

Cross a footbridge at the bottom of the
third pond, about 800m from the car park,
to follow the waymarked path to the left
which heads uphill before levelling out:
keep to the widest path with high earthen
banks on each side and ignore the stile
and path leading off to the left about
250m further on.

At a junction after another 500m, bear
left to follow the path next to a fence.
This joins a wider track which you follow
round to the left a few metres ahead.
After passing a couple of houses, turn
right at the crossroads of bridleways and
continue straight on through another
crossroads in about 150m.

Where the path emerges from woodland

◄ Ludshott Common

to join a sandy path, continue straight ahead and stay on the widest path. The sandy nutrient-poor soil found here provides the perfect conditions for wild bilberry, heather, Scots pine and birch to grow. Continue on this sandy path, avoiding more minor routes leading off it, until you arrive at a junction marked by a bench, where you turn right.

After 1km, you pass another bench and emerge at a T-junction, where you turn right. There are several paths leading off at various points: stay on the widest path, which is mostly sandy. The path swings round to the right to shortly head southwestwards before it splits just ahead. Continue straight on at the junction and bear left at the next fork.

At a junction of paths in around 400m, carry straight on into woodland and soon go left onto a less-used path which passes under some powerlines and in a short time is intersected by a vehicle track. Cross this and keep going straight ahead, passing some upright posts in the ground which prevent vehicle access.

In another 50m, you cross another vehicle track and pass under the powerlines again. After a further 300m, continue straight ahead at the crossroads of paths. On meeting a minor public road (Waggoners Wells Lane), bear right to follow it back to the car park.

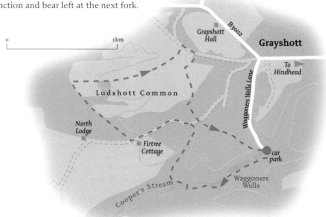

Petersfield

Distance 6km **Time** 2 hours
Terrain paths along field edges, across a
meadow and through hangers; initially
flat but becomes hilly with some very
steep sections **Map** OS Explorer OL33
Access buses from Winchester, Havant,
Chichester and Horndean; trains from
London and Portsmouth; lay-by parking
available at the start of the walk

This bracing walk will get the heart
pumping. The reward for ascending some
particularly steep hills is a fantastic view
to the south and the chance to see the
interior of a hanger, peculiar to this part
of Hampshire. Hangers tend to be
comprised mostly of beech and are
usually ancient woodland sites.

From the small lay-by on Bell Hill,
which connects the A3 with Petersfield,
head downhill on the pavement for a few
metres, then turn right onto a lane next
to a red postbox. At the end of the lane,

follow the footpath that swings left, then
turn right to cross an overpass of the A3.
Turn immediately right after going
through a gate on the other side of the
overpass to cross a series of four fields
accessed via stiles on a waymarked route.

Cross an asphalt driveway and continue
straight ahead on the waymarked path.
When you meet a minor public road about
150m further on, turn briefly left before
bearing right into a field containing a
variety of wildflower and grass species.

Follow the path across this and along
the margin in the next field. Keep an eye
out for an old watertank to your left.
When level with the tank, take the path to
the right which heads steeply uphill
between fields. Impressive views are the
reward for your effort.

At the top of the steep field, enter the
woodland (Ashford Hangers National
Nature Reserve) and continue up a flight
of steps. After climbing sharply, the

◀ Curious lambs at Petersfield

route exits the woodland and follows a faint path straight ahead to the top of the field, where you join the minor public road and take the left branch at the fork just ahead, signposted as a dead-end road. Just beyond a cottage the road becomes an unsurfaced lane. Around 600m after this point, you encounter a waymarker next to a series of upright wooden posts. Here, you turn left to descend a very steep track through woodland (Lythe Hanger).

At the bottom of the track turn left to continue downhill. Just beyond a memorial bench carry on along a minor road until you reach the entrance of Lythe Farm. Here, bear left across the farm driveway and go over a stile to join a waymarked path across a series of fields. Sections of the fences in these fields can be unclipped to allow pedestrian access and reattached behind you.

After passing in front of the large farmhouse at Soal Farm, you walk through a copse and across another series of fields. The path is faint, but the route is easy to spot due to the gaps in the hedges between the fields. After crossing a small

wooden footbridge, bear right onto the vague path, which leads to a minor road.

Cross the road and continue straight ahead on the track opposite, heading uphill. Just after passing Cooks Cottage, go over the stile on your right into a field and continue straight ahead for another 600m, crossing several fields. In each of these, aim for the gap in the hedge which marks the location of a stile.

At the bottom of the final field, go over a stile to join a fenced-off strip, where you bear left. The noise of traffic clearly indicates the presence of the dual carriageway. Continue to the overpass and from there retrace your route to the start.

Butser Hill

Distance 2.5km **Time** 1 hour
Terrain faint, gently undulating paths
around the grassy summit of Butser Hill
Map OS Explorer OL8 **Access** no public
transport to the start; car park available
at the start of the walk

At 271m Butser Hill is the second highest
top in Hampshire (after Pilot Hill), the
second highest point in the South Downs
National Park and the second largest area
of calcareous grassland in Hampshire.
It is also a National Nature Reserve with
expansive views and, in summer, flitting
butterflies and trilling skylarks.

Butser Hill is classified as a Marilyn,
meaning an upward protuberance greater
than 150m. The term 'Marilyn' was coined
in 1992 and is a pun on the famous
Scottish mountain classification of
Munros, whose summits rise above 914m.

From the Butser Hill car park, take the
track that heads uphill and passes the
public toilets. After going through a
pedestrian access gate, bear right and
follow the asphalt track towards a radio
mast and buildings.

Where the track swerves left towards
the base of the mast and buildings,
continue straight ahead on the grassy
track, passing a clump of hawthorn
bushes. As you head towards the trig
point marking the summit of the hill, the
fantastic 360° views will stop you in your
tracks. A patchwork of fields stitched
together with hedges and deciduous
woodland copses stretching to the
distance makes this a truly impressive
sight and it is one of south England's
most popular paragliding and hang-
gliding sites.

Butser Hill's flat summit is surrounded

by several spurs. Iron Age ditches and banks divide the spurs from the summit, although their original purpose is unclear. Roman pottery has been dug up by rabbits, but no thorough excavations have been carried out. It is apparent, however, that Butser Hill has a commanding presence over the surrounding countryside and was obviously a site of great strategic importance.

To the south of the hill is Butser Ancient Farm, a unique recreation of a working farm from the pre-Roman Iron Age, about 2400 years ago. The farm is a research project that tests ideas which have been developed from discoveries made during many archaeological excavations across Britain. Research at the site, which includes breeding direct descendants of Iron Age domestic animals and growing crops from strains known to be in use in prehistory, has elucidated that Iron Age farmers were accomplished land and stock managers.

Continue beyond the trig point and follow the faint path around the rim of the summit, which is fairly flat. Wooden posts marked with red paint indicate a circular route, although the cattle which graze the hilltop tend to use them

as scratching posts and frequently flatten them. When you reach the northwest point of the plateau, with Ramsdean Down beneath you, swing left to continue. The views to the west are great in any clear weather, but catching a sunset from here can be spectacular. Continue south until you meet the vehicle track to the mast that you followed earlier. From here, retrace your steps to the car park.

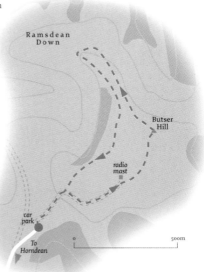

◄ View from the summit of Butser Hill

89

Farlington Marshes

Distance 4.5km **Time** 1 hour 30
Terrain level paths around a grassy
promontory **Map** OS Explorer OL8
Access no public transport to the start;
car parks at the start of the walk

**This nature reserve, managed by the
Hampshire and Isle of Wight Wildlife
Trust, offers wonderful walks all year
round, but during the winter it really
comes to life, playing host to a
staggering number of migratory
overwintering wildfowl.**

Farlington Marshes is accessed via an
easily missed narrow driveway on the
busy A27 exit just as it comes off the
Farlington Interchange roundabout
between Portsmouth and Havant: it's on
the opposite side of the roundabout from
a Holiday Inn Express. If the first car parks
accessed off the driveway are full, or you

want to park closer to the start of the
walk, continue along the track as there is
a smaller parking area at the start of the
path which leads into the reserve.

The reserve is an area of about 120
hectares of land in Langstone Harbour
that was reclaimed in 1771 for grazing
purposes, and it features both freshwater
marsh and brackish marsh. Cattle are still
grazed here for conservation purposes.

During the Second World War Farlington
Marshes was used as a 'starfish site' for
Portsmouth, located just to the west on
Portsea Island. Starfish sites were decoys
that consisted of light systems and fires
controlled from a nearby bunker and were
laid out to simulate a fire-bombed town.
It was hoped that these decoys would
encourage German pilots to think that the
city or town had already been bombed, so
that they would then drop their bombs in

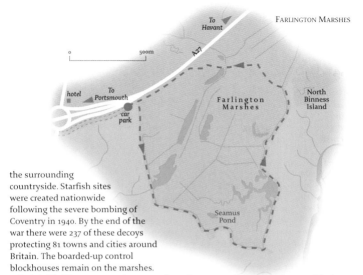

the surrounding countryside. Starfish sites were created nationwide following the severe bombing of Coventry in 1940. By the end of the war there were 237 of these decoys protecting 81 towns and cities around Britain. The boarded-up control blockhouses remain on the marshes.

Dark-bellied Brent geese, wigeons, teals, avocets, redshanks and dunlins flock to Farlington Marshes in their thousands in winter. However, it is pleasant at any time of year, with views across the sandflats at Langstone Harbour at low tide. During the spring and summer migrations, the reserve becomes a hotspot for warblers, redstarts, spotted flycatchers, wrynecks, wheatears and whinchats, while lapwings, redshanks, meadow pipits and skylarks breed on the marshes. Rafts have been placed on some of the ponds within the reserve to provide nesting habitats for terns. If you have some binoculars, you'll enjoy watching the terns and other birds on these ponds and on the narrow channels that connect them.

A kissing gate at the end of the final car park gives access to a path leading into the reserve. An information panel just beyond the kissing gate details the recent bird sightings. Just after the information panel, bear right onto the path which runs along the reserve's perimeter. This trail is exposed to wind and sea spray, so on gusty days at full tide expect an exhilarating walk. Follow the path around the promontory for about 3km to reach a pair of sturdy gateposts at a slight curve in the perimeter wall. Here, you bear left onto a wide stony track. At the path junction about 25m ahead, bear left onto a wide unmetalled vehicle track.

Shortly after, you pass the former bunker that was used to control the light and pyrotechnic displays when this was a starfish site. After 450m the track joins a cycletrack, where you bear left to return to the start.

◀ Farlington Marshes are a haven for wildlife

West Harting Down

Distance 7.5km **Time** 2 hours 30
Terrain unsurfaced lanes and forest
tracks, undulating but none particularly
steep **Map** OS Explorer OL8 **Access** no
public transport to the start; no on-street
parking is available; if you intend to visit
the Red Lion you may park in the pub car
park at the landlord's discretion, or it's
5km by bike (on road) from Finchdean

West Harting Down is named after a
medieval hunting ground where the
prized deer stag – commonly known
as a hart – was flushed by hounds
towards nobles and clergy, who waited in
ambush at the periphery of long glades.
The Normans were particularly fond of
recreational stag hunting. The most
sought-after prize was a white hart.

The thatched and timber-framed Red
Lion is thought to be the oldest pub in
Hampshire and its cosy bar area includes
an original inglenook fireplace. Opposite
the pub is the Church of St Michael and
All Angels, which is of early Norman
design and built on the site of an older
Anglo-Saxon church. The church's font
was vandalised during the English civil
war in the mid-17th century.

When exiting the Red Lion's car park,
turn left, then bear immediate right at the
road junction just ahead. Follow this road
past the former post office, after which
you turn right to head uphill. Continue
past Manor Farm and ignore the
waymarked byway.

Just past the byway, turn left onto a
footpath at an easy-to-miss waymarker.
This is part of the Sussex Border Path and
Staunton Way long-distance routes. After
descending steeply through a couple of
fields you meet a minor road, where you

bear left before shortly turning right to cross a railway line via an overpass.

A few metres beyond the overpass cross the driveway to Ditcham Park School and join an unmetalled lane next to the gate lodge. Just ahead is a junction, where you continue straight ahead on the lowest of the three routes, waymarked as the Sussex Border Path.

The path passes through young woodland, and at a gravel lorry turning area you continue straight ahead on the wide waymarked bridleway, ignoring paths leading off from it. At a fork about 2km after entering the woodland, bear left to follow the broad grassy forest access route which is level at this point.

At another fork 350m ahead, bear left to follow a narrow footpath into the trees. The waymarker is just inside the woodland. Bear left at another waymarker a few

metres ahead. When the path meets a field fence, turn left to follow the path steeply uphill next to the fence.

At the top of the field the path levels off. After about 100m the path joins a driveway which you follow for 300m to arrive at the gates of Ditcham Park School. Here, you bear left to join a waymarked footpath heading downhill adjacent to the school's driveway. Follow this path for around 2km to the gate lodge to Ditcham Park School, which you walked past earlier. Retrace your footsteps to the start of the route from here.

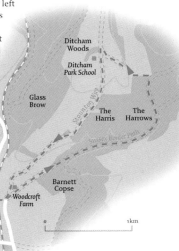

Selborne

Distance 7.5km **Time** 2 hours 30
Terrain woodland paths, some very
steep sections but manageable with
a moderate level of fitness
Map OS Explorer OL33 **Access** buses
from Alton, Petersfield, Horndean and
Clanfield; car park at the start of the walk

Selborne lies within the South Downs
National Park and was the home of the
famous 18th-century naturalist Gilbert
White whose 1789 book *The Natural
History and Antiquities of Selborne* was
continuously in print for more than 200
years. White's former residence, the
impressive The Wakes, is now a museum.

From the car park next to the Selborne
Arms just off the main village street, take
the path next to the public toilets. From
here, the route leads gently uphill to meet
the entrance to Selborne Common.

Bear left at the information panel and
climb steeply uphill on the zigzag path.

A bench halfway up the hill provides a
rest stop with a great view. Continue
the climb on the path just to the left of
the bench.

After passing a yew tree near the top of
the hill, turn right, then bear right at the
bench just beyond to continue uphill to a
field gate. Go through the gate to traverse
Selborne Hill and continue straight ahead
on the wide grassy path.

At a fork in around 850m, bear left and
carry on to a crossroads of waymarked
paths, where you continue straight ahead
downhill. After about 200m, go through
the gate to leave Selborne Common and
join Green Lane, a track with banked sides
that indicate its antiquity. The track bears
south from the gate and leaves the
woodland to continue between fields to
an asphalt road.

Cross this and continue straight ahead
on the route opposite, which leads
diagonally across a field via an unplanted